MW01118825

"Simply Elegant"

A guide for elegant but simple entertaining

by

Pearl Sgutt Gordon

First Printing, March 1970
Second Printing, August 1970
Third Printing, Revised Edition, December 1971
Fourth Printing, March 1972
Fifth Printing, November 1972
Sixth Printing, Revised Edition, December 1975
Seventh Printing, Revised Edition, January 1978
Eighth Printing, Revised Edition, 1981
Ninth Printing, Revised Edition, 1984
Tenth Printing, Revised Edition, 1984

Printed in United States of America

Simply Elegant
4562 14th Way NE
St Petersburg, FL 33703

To my dear husband, Marvin
and our sons, Charles Mark,
James Brian,
and Evan Sgutt

"If we could pick our Mothers
Like flowers in a row
I'd pursue a pair of scissors,
        a basket, and a hoe
I would choose the fairest blooming
the finest I could find
And cultivate and nourish it
        the rarest of its kind.
A darling is my Mother
the most precious ever known
She is like a flower
the most perfect ever grown."

Pearl Sgutt Gordon

A bouquet of thanks to my Mother, Fanny Sgutt Gordon.

"Simply Elegant"

The Author, Pearl Sgutt Gordon

Family and friends have been kind in asking me to write this book. I hope all who read "SIMPLY ELEGANT" will find it a helpful guide to elegant but simple entertaining.

Casual simple ways of informal entertaining are wonderful, but intersperse them with formal, glamorous, old-fashioned ways, too.

Times have changed, and we no longer have maids or just the housewife cooking. College boys, brides and dads in mind, I have tried to make "SIMPLY ELEGANT" a concise, easy to follow book of my treasured recipes and ideas for entertaining.

Happy eating!

Pearl S. Gordon

TABLE OF CONTENTS

THE ELEGANT DINNER TABLE

Everyone loves to have dinner at an elegant dinner table. The crystal chandelier is turned down to very dim lights. The gleaming linen dinner cloth and napkins are freshly laundered. The fresh flowers in your centerpiece blend in with the lit tapers in your candelabra.

At each person's place at the table the silverware is shined and meticulously set. The service plates, the crystal goblets and wine glasses are placed in proper order.

The maid sets the first course on the service plate.

If the host is to serve, the serving cart is placed next to him, and the food is on it in chafing dishes and large serving pieces.

The maid removes the service plates and first course and exchanges them for the second course. As the host carves and fills the plates, the maid serves them to each guest.

The climax of the dinner occurs when the dishes are all removed and a regal dessert is brought in to top off the delicious dinner. The dessert and dessert plates are placed in front of the hostess to serve.

The dinner is completed when the guests are served demi tasse or after dinner drinks to sip in the living room.

My favorite formal dinner guests are my very own children.

A WINE TASTING PARTY

A Wine Tasting Party is exciting any afternoon or evening. Wines, a fabulous assortment of cheeses, exotic breads, a copious bowl of fruit, and even very thinly sliced meat, should grace the table. On the table, with the wine glasses, should be a waste bowl to empty the wine glass into, if needed, and fruit knives and little plates.

A yardstick loaf of French bread that guests may break off chunks and then select cheese to accompany it, is fun. Fresh figs, quartered and peeled, New Zealand green apples, or any tart apples, pears and chunks of melons are divine. Melon balls are delicious with very thinly sliced meat wrapped around them.

Select no more than six wines. Commence with dry white wines and the lightest wines first, and end with the red dessert wines. For example:
Dry White Wine . . . Riesling
German Moselle
White Burgundy
Cabernet Sauvignon
Zinfandel
Red Burgundy

Open the still wines an hour before serving. Do not open sparkling wines until the moment of pouring. Serve white wines and rosés cold, sparkling red or white wines, icy cold, and red wines at room temperature. There are many different cheeses to choose from:

Bel Paese	Brie	Camembert	Cheddar	Cremé Chantilly
Gorgonzola	Gruyére	Liederkranz	Mel Fino	Merovingian
Oka	Pont L'Eveque	Edam	Poona	Port Du Salut
Emmenthal				

Browsing at wine and cheese stores, will help you with your selections for your party.

TIME FOR TEA

The tea table is set with your best party cloth, organdy and linen in the spring and summer, or linen cut work for fall and winter.

The flowers go with the season and depend on what type of cloth you are using. The flower color scheme is carried out in the candy and also in the sugar crystals in your sugar bowl.

The coffee service is at one end of the table, and your largest silver tray filled with tiny sandwiches is at the opposite end of the table. Tea cakes and tiny cookies fill in the table.

INFORMAL BUFFET DINNER

Informal dinner parties are fun for all. The hostess can be relaxed when the buffet table is set and ready to serve.

Gay table linens with fine china, crystal, and sterling are in order. Match your casual table linens with pottery, pewter, or stainless steel. Copper and brass, combined or separate, lend their tone to bright linens. Blend your centerpiece and the color scheme together on your buffet table.

Barbecueing is great for an informal buffet and the men can help cook. Anything goes for this type of dinner party. Have a large table set for your guests or several small tables. Dessert may be served at the dinner table with coffee.

COCKTAIL DINNERS

A pleasant prelude, with cocktails, to a cocktail dinner are hot hors d'oeuvres.

Later the guests adjourn to the dining room candlelit buffet table and help themselves. For a cocktail dinner, place the meat on the table with small sandwich rolls near by, and let the guests make their own sandwiches. Serve food that the guests may eat easily either standing or sitting.

Coffee is served later with cake or much later in the evening with schnecken (rich cinnamon rolls).

COCKTAIL SUPPER

A cocktail supper is a more simple way to entertain glamorously.

The buffet table is set up so that the guests may nibble and drink all evening while they visit. Bitesize sandwiches, already made, are on the table along with hot food in chafing dishes. Much later in the evening coffee and schnecken are set out for the guests to help themselves.

COFFEE TIME

A coffee party is one of the easiest ways to entertain. Guests drop over in casual attire to "visit" and enjoy "a cup of coffee."

The buffet table is set with casual linens, coffee, of course, fresh fruits, in season, cinnamon rolls and coffee cakes.

The time for a "coffee" is usually 10:00 a.m. to 12:00 noon.

The afternoon coffee party is different because you serve different food. Coffee cake is still in order, but cheese cake, cookies, cakes and tortes are served.

LUNCHEONS

Luncheons may be at seated tables or buffet style. The food served at a luncheon should be light. Warm foods should be served in cold weather and cool foods, such as salads, in warm weather.

Scrumptious desserts add the touch of elegance to a lovely afternoon.

CHILDREN'S LOVES

Babies love:
Eggs scrambled with a little milk in a double boiler. They are so light and fluffy.

Little children love:
Milk toast. Butter toast and tear into pieces. Place in a bowl and cover with warm milk and add a little sugar.

Little children with no appetites love:
A Toast Man. A rounded top banana slice for the head. A round slice of orange, peeled, for the tummy. Buttered toast for arms and legs. Eyes, nose, mouth and buttons are made of raisins.

Little ones that won't drink milk love:
Playing elevator, and their milk disappears fast. A full glass of milk is the 10th floor. Call out the floors as the milk goes down until they "hit the basement." The milk is all gone!

Children with coughs love:
Hot milk and rock candy (or honey) heated in it and a lump of butter melted in it.

Thin children love:
Eggnogs. In blender or mixer, mix together: Milk, eggs, sugar and vanilla. Beat well and serve topped with nutmeg.

Little children love:
Parties with candy hunts. Give each child a paper sack with his name on it. Let them gather all the wrapped soft candies that you have sprinkled or hidden in an area. The one who finds the least amount wins the prize.

Big children love:
Bubble gum and peanut hunts at parties.

All children love:
Oatmeal with a lump of butter, brown sugar and cream.

Little children love:
A miniature pie for themselves when Mommy makes a large pie for adults.

Little children love:
Hot cereal with raisins that make a face.

Little children love:
Sandwiches in the shapes of animals. Cut shapes of animals with your large cooky cutters.

Children love:
French toast cut (by cutters) in the shapes of dolls. Use boy and girl cutters.

Little children love:
Choo choo train cakes. Slice a loaf angel food cake into 3 layers. Fill layers with ice cream. Frost cake with whipped cream that is tinted the color you desire and flavored accordingly. Decorate with gumdrops.

Children love:
Cookies made in the shapes of animals and a little man.

Teenagers love:
Individual pizzas. Take small rolls or small English muffins. Spread each half with tomato sauce or pizza ketchup. On top of this add hamburger (that has been browned in the skillet). You may add green pepper pieces, mushrooms or whatever you desire. Sprinkle Mozarella cheese over this or a slice of Swiss cheese and broil. Serve hot.

Teenagers love:
Baked Alaska in flower pots. When done baking add a plastic flower on top.

Teenagers love:
After ice skating parties or football games, hot cocoa and marshmallows. This is for one person: Heat 1 cup milk in saucepan. In a cup mix 1 scant teaspoon cocoa and 2 scant teaspoons sugar. Add a little milk to the cocoa mixture, and make a paste. Stir this into milk in pan and let it come to a boil. Watch it very closely and immediately when it boils, remove from stove and pour it into a cup that already contains marshmallows, serve immediately.

What to do with extra —

EGG YOLKS

Blintzes
Mayonnaise
Butter Cookies
Chocolate Pinwheel Cookies
Chocolate Cream Pie
Chocolate Rum Torte
Pots de Creme
Strawberry Cream Flan
Chocolate Rum Cake
Fresh Pineapple in Hot Rum
Banana Cream Pie
Hot Cheese Puffs
Toffee Bars
Spritz Cookies

SOUR CREAM

Sour Cream Drop Cookies
Cheese with Kuchen Dough
Chocolate Sour Cream Cake
Croissants
Date Cake
Peaches 'n' Cream Coffee Cake
Sour Cream Coffee Cake
Lemon Coffee Bread
Kugel #1
Schnecken
Blueberry Coffee Cake
Orange Tea Wafers
Sour Cream Plum Torte
Sour Cream Bundt Cake
Banana Bread

EGG WHITES

Angel Food Cake
Chocolate Angel Food Cake
Vacherin
White Cake
Marshmallow Frosting
Heavenly Pie
Chocolate Mocha Angel Pie
Chocolate Candy Pie
Snow Peak Frosting
Elegant Party Torte
Meringue Shells or Nests
Brown Sugar Orange Frosting
Divinity
Meringue Mushrooms

Menus

MENUS

Index

CHAMPAGNE BUFFET DINNER

Champagne

Roulé de Caviar   Hot Chicken Livers

Swiss Crab Gordon in Shells

Party Rye

Relish Tray
of
Artichoke Hearts, Cherry Tomatoes,
Green & Ripe Olives, Marinated Asparagus & Tiny Carrots

Whole Baked Fresh Salmon

Filet of Beef Bordeaux   Roast Turkey

Breads

Hot Fruit Compote   Potato Salad

Chocolate Rum Torte   Rum Chocolate Trifle

Coffee

COCKTAIL SUPPER

Cocktails

Tiny Turkey Sandwiches   Chopped Chicken Livers

Party Rye

Lobster Thermidor in Sea Shells

Cherry Tomatoes   Brussels Sprouts
Stuffed with cream cheese & chives

Lemon-Orange Meringue Tarts   Sour Cream Plum Torte

Coffee

AFTER THE GAME SUPPER

Cheese Spread

Crackers

Janet's Gantse Tsimas

Light Butter Lettuce Salad

Crusty Bread   Sweet Butter

Dark Beer

or

Robust Red Burgundy

Lemon-Orange Pie   Coffee

BOY'S BIRTHDAY DINNER

8 to 12 year olds

Tomato Juice

Hamburgers   Buns

French Fried Potatoes

Ice Cream Balls

or

Tapioca Pudding

Topped with Whipped Cream & Gumdrops

Birthday Cake

Milk

Table Decorations:

Blue placemats. Red and white napkins.
Centerpiece of 2 small baseball bats,
2 styrofoam balls decorated with red
markings to look like baseballs. Miniature
baseball team players on birthday cake.

SUMMER BUFFET

Eggs Stuffed with Caviar

or

Eggs Stuffed with Sardines

(Skinless, boneless sardines mashed with
lemon juice, mayonnaise, grated onion and
ketchup)

Cold Sliced Corned Beef   Cold Sliced Tongue

Tomatoes Stuffed with Cole Slaw

Brown Rice and Mushrooms

Pumpernickel   Light Rye Breads

Shell of Fruit

with

Pear and Peach Halves, Strawberries
Honeydew Melon and Cantaloupe slices
Bananas and Fresh Pineapple
Sprinkle Sherry and Confectioners' Sugar

Chocolate Pound Cake

Elegant Brandy Bundt Cake

Coffee

SUMMER LUNCHEON

Cold White Wine

Tossed Green Salad   Swiss Cheese Quiche

Hot French Bread

Fresh Fruit   Orange Marble Cake

21

BRUNCH

Bloody Marys

Scrambled Eggs with Chicken Livers or Mushrooms

Fresh Fruit (in season)   Broiled Tomatoes

Cheese Blintzes

Cherry Preserves   Sour Cream

Cinnamon Rolls   Coffee Cake

Coffee

COCKTAIL DINNER

Coquille St. Jacques

Tossed Green Salad

Croissants

Charcoal Broiled Tenderloin

Artichoke Bottoms Filled with pureed or tiny peas

Potato Souffle   Hot Fruit Compote

Lemon-Orange Filled Pots de Creme

Coffee

SWEET SIXTEEN BIRTHDAY LUNCHEON

Fruit Punch

Albacore Tuna Salad on Pinneapple Rings

Cold Marinated Asparagus   Orange Muffins

Elegant Party Torte

Ice Tea   Milk

LUNCHEON

Sherry

Chicken ala king in patty shells

Fresh Broccoli   Spiced Peaches

Hot Rolls   Preserves

Chocolate Rum Cake (Icebox)

Coffee

LUNCHEON

Sherry

Avocado Filled with Crab Salad

Spiced Peach

Fresh Buttered Asparagus   Hot Cinnamon Rolls

Vacherin or Chocolate Rum Torte

Coffee

SUMMER LUNCHEON

Gazpacho

Individual Salmon Mousse

White Asparagus   Tiny Belgium Carrots

Croissants

Sweet Butter   Strawberry Jam

Blueberry Pie with Homemade Ice Cream

Coffee   Iced Tea

DINNER

Chopped Chicken Livers   Herring in Wine Sauce

Crackers and Party Rye   Relishes

Tossed Salad

Leg o'Lamb

Browned Potatoes   Fresh Broccoli

Baked Peaches with Mint Jelly

Dinner Rolls

Elegant Party Torte

or

Chocolate Cake with Fudge Frosting

Coffee

DINNER

Sweet and Sour Shrimp   Marcella's Hot Clam Spread

Cinnamon Apple Salad

Brisket a la Gordon

Parsleyed New Potatoes   Buttered New Peas

Hot Rolls

Mousse au Chocolat in Pots de Creme Cups

Coffee

DINNER

Cream Cheese & Caviar   Crabmeat Cheese Dip

Crackers & Potato Chips

Relishes

Salad
of

Lettuce, Sliced Tomato, White
Asparagus & Artichoke Hearts

Prime Rib Roast

Browned Potatoes   Buttered Peas

Hot Rolls   Preserves

Blueberry Pie or Mocha Angel Pie

Coffee

ITALIAN DINNER

Italian Wine

Tossed Salad with Italian Dressing

Spaghetti with Meat or Shrimp

Italian Green Beans   Hot Garlic Bread

Cantaloupe Rings filled with Ice Cream

Sugar Cookie on Top

Coffee

FALL DINNER

Red Wine

Chicken in Orange Shells

Salad of Lettuce, Tomato & Caviar

Hot Rolls   Peach Preserves

Apple Stuffed Veal Rolls

Fresh Broccoli

Orange Marshmallow Mold

Burnt Sugar Chiffon Cake   Coffee

THANKSGIVING DINNER

Swiss Olivets

Chopped Chicken Livers

Crackers   Party Rye

Relish Tray   Hot Rolls

Roast Turkey

Dressing   Mashed Potatoes & Gravy

Candied Yams

Green Beans with Almonds   Cranberry Mold

Warm Apple Pie   Coffee

BUFFET DINNER

Tiny Swiss Cheese Quiches   Stuffed Mushrooms

Tossed Green Salad

Orange Pineapple Mold

with

Cream cheese stuffed whole apricots
Pineapple chunks, pear halves and
Maraschino cherries

Baked Fresh Salmon

Lemon wedges & Tartar Sauce

Escalloped Potatoes   Buttered New Peas

Muffins

Chocolate Mocha Cake with Coffee Icing

Coffee

TEENAGERS DINNER PARTY

Crabmeat Cheese Dip   Potato Chips

Tossed Salad   Apricot Ring

Garlic Broiled Chicken Paprikash

Corn on the Cob   Potatoes & Onions

Muffins

Chocolate Buttermilk Cake with Fudge Frosting

Milk   Soft Drinks

WINE TASTING PARTY

Fresh Fruit

Chopped Herring   Rye Bread

Cheese
    Danish Cream Havarti (Dofino)
    Baby Swiss
    Port Salut
    Brie
Assorted Crackers

Wine
    Pouilly-fuisse
    Beaujolais
    Cabernet Sauvignon
    Zinfandel

Elegant Brandy Bundt Cake
Chocolate Pound Cake

Coffee

WINTER BUFFET

Wheel of Cheese   Crackers

Marinated white & green asparagus, baby carrots,
artichoke hearts, & green beans

Poached Salmon in Aspic   Cucumber Dill Sauce

Brown Rice and Mushrooms

Croissants   Sweet Butter   Strawberry Preserves

Shell of fresh pineapple, pear & peach halves, apricots
Sprinkle with sherry and confectioners sugar

Coffee

Hot Bread Pudding Souffle
Brandy Sauce

Divinity   Salted Nuts

Hors D'oeuvres

HORS D'OEUVRES

Index

ROULÉ de CAVIAR

1. Melt **1/2 stick butter** in pan, and gradually stir in **1/2 cup flour.** Slowly stir in **2 cups milk,** and cook, stirring constantly, until mixture boils. Turn burner down, still stirring, to simmer until thick.

2. Beat **4 egg yolks** well. Add a little hot sauce to the beaten yolks, then blend yolks with the hot sauce. Stir in **1 tsp. sugar.**

3. Beat **4 egg whites** until stiff. Fold them into the mixutre.

4. Line a greased 10 by 15 inch loaf cake pan with waxed paper that has been also greased and lightly floured. Spread batter into pan and bake in 325 degree oven for about 40 to 45 minutes, until it is golden brown and springs back at your touch. Turn out onto aluminum foil or tea towel.

Filling:

1. Whip softened **cream cheese (6 ounces),** with **1/4 cup sour cream.** Add **four ounces caviar,** squeeze in a little **lemon juice,** and mix. Spread gently on turned out cake.

2. Roll cake like a jelly roll.

3. Place on a narrow tray and slice thinly.

SWISS OLIVETS

1. Cut small rounds of **white bread.**
2. Spread **butter or margarine** on top of each round and place on cookie sheet.

3. Spoon **chopped ripe olives** on each bread round.

4. Dot each round with **salad dressing.**

5. Top rounds with **Swiss cheese.**

6. Refrigerate until ready to use.

7. Broil until cheese bubbles. Serve immediately.

CHOPPED ONIONS AND EGGS

1. Chop **2 onions** very fine. Add **8 hard cooked eggs** and continue chopping.

2. Add **4 Tbsp. rendered chicken fat, salt** and **pepper** to taste. Mix well. Serve with **rye bread.**

CHOPPED CHICKEN LIVERS

1. Broil or bake **chicken livers.**

2. Grind in meatgrinder or in blender: livers, **hard boiled eggs, onion.** When all are blended together, place in bowl and season with **salt** and a little **pepper.**

3. Add **chicken fat.** (Take the fat from a chicken and wash and place in a kettle with an onion that has been quartered. Cook until fat is all melted. Strain fat into glass container.)

4. After livers have been mixed, place on a plate in a mound. Serve with party rye bread or crackers. Eggs separated after they have been boiled may be used after they have been chopped, for decorative purposes. Place yolks on top and the whites around the edge.

STUFFED RYE

1. Hollow out **round rye** or pumpernickel. Reserve bread and cut in small pieces.

2. Fill center of bread with **chopped chicken livers** and place sliced bread around it.

SWISS CHEESE QUICHE

1. In mixing bowl beat **3 eggs** well, then **1 3/4 cups milk** or cream. Add **1/2 tsp. salt, dash of white pepper, dash of nutmeg, 2 Tbsp. very soft** or **melted butter.** Blend well.

2. Stir in **1 cup grated Swiss cheese.**

3. If you desire, you may stir in **cut up lobster** or **shrimp** and add a little **sherry.**

4. Pour into an 8 inch partially baked pastry shell or tart or tartlet shells for tiny hors d'oeuvres.

5. Bake at 375° for 30 minutes, if making a large quiche, in the upper third of your oven. Bake less for small quiches.

6. Quiche is done when it has puffed and browned. A knife inserted in the center should come out clean.

7. It will stay puffed for 10 minutes in turned off oven with door ajar. It may be reheated and eaten either hot or cold.

potato sal-
s and mari-

1. Thanksgiving dinner. Roast turkey with dressing, candied yams in chafing dish, cranberries, and olives.

2. Dessert Table. Clockwise, L to R: Orange Marble Cake, Little Children's apple pie, Blueberry Pie, Elegant Party Torte, Old Fashioned Cheese Cake, Elegant Brandy Bundt Cake, Apple Pie, Chocolate Rum Torte, and Delicate Lemon Bars.

3. Dinner for four. Leg O Lamb, browned potatoes, peaches baked with mint jelly.

4. A pleasant prelude for dinner are hot hor d'oeuvres.
   Roule' de Caviar   Swiss Olivets
   Swiss Crab Gordon in Shells.

5. Luncheon table. Crabmeat salad in an avocado, pineapple slice and hot rolls.

6. Little children love a toast man and hot cereal with raisins that make a face.

Photo Appearing On The Front of Foldout:

My favorite formal dinner guests are my very own childr

Photo Appearing On The Back of Foldout:

Informal buffet in the library. Whole baked fresh salmo
ad, hot fruit compote, relish tray of artichoke hearts, pi
nated asparagus spears, and brisket ala Gordon.

CHICKEN IN ORANGE SHELLS

1. Combine **2 cups cooked breast of chicken** finely diced, **3/4 cup mayonnaise, juice** and **grated rind** of **1 orange** and a **dash of salt** and **pepper.**

2. Cut **4 oranges** in half. Remove a thin slice from each bottom so that shells will sit properly. Remove pulp. Inside of shell should be clean and white.

3. Fill each shell with chicken mixture. Chill before serving. Garnish with sprig of parsley and orange sections.

HOT CLAM SPREAD

1. In a double boiler melt **1 eight ounce pkg. cream cheese,** add a little **onion juice, worcestershire sauce, salt** and **pepper** and **chives.**

2. When melted, add **1 can minced clams.**

3. If mixture is too thick, add **clam juice** until right consistency to use for dip with potato chips.

4. Serve hot in chafing dish.

SWISS CRAB GORDON IN SHELLS

1. Lightly butter or spray with vegetable spray each shell.

2. Sprinkle **1 cup (4 ounces) shredded Swiss cheese** evenly over bottom of each shell.

3. Sprinkle **crabmeat,** that has been flaked (fresh, frozen, or canned, about half a pound) over cheese.

4. Slice **2 green onions** (tops and all) thinly over crabmeat.

5. In a small bowl combine **3 beaten eggs, 1 cup light cream, dash of salt 1/2 grated lemon peel, 1/4 tsp. dry mustard,** and a **dash of mace.** Add a little **sherry** for flavor. Mix well and spoon over ingredients in shells.

6. Bake at 325 degrees for 15 or 20 minutes, on cookie sheets.

7. Remove from oven and let stand until shells are cool enough to serve. Serve with cocktail forks.

SMOKED WHITE FISH SPREAD

1. Soften **one 3 oz. pkg. cream cheese** with **sour cream.**

2. Add a little **grated onion,** a **dash** of **salt** and **worcestershire sauce.**

3. De-bone completely **2 chubs (white fish)** and add to above.

4. Serve as spread with tiny slices of **pumpernickel.** If "smoked" taste is too strong, add more cheese.

CRABMEAT CHEESE DIP

1. Whip with fork **one 8 oz. pkg. cream cheese** that has been standing at room temperature for several hours. Add enough milk to thin for dipping.

2. Add **worcestershire sauce, onion juice** and **flakes** of **1 can** of **crabmeat.**

3. Mix well and place in dip bowl. Serve with potato chips.

CHEESE SPREAD

1. Blend together: a **3 oz.** and **8 oz. pkg. cream cheese, 4 oz. cold pack blue cheese, 10 oz. sharp** (or Nippy) **cheese,** very finely grate in a little onion. Add **1/2 cup chopped pecans.** Mix well together.

2. Before serving, sprinkle with **paprika.** Serve on cheese board with crackers.

SMOKED SALMON CHEESE BALL

1. Drain and remove bones from one **1 lb. can** of **red Alaska salmon.**

2. Flake salmon and add **one 8 oz.** very soft **pkg.** of **cream cheese, 1 Tbsp. lemon juice, 2 tsp. grated onion, 1 tsp. prepared horseradish** and **1/4 tsp. liquid smoke.** Mix thoroughly.

3. Chill for several hours.

4. Shape into ball and roll in snipped parsley. Serve with crackers.

COQUILLE ST. JACQUES

1. Wash and drain well **2 lbs.** of scallops, place in a saucepan with **2 cups dry white wine, 2 sprigs of parsley, sprig of thyme,** and a **bay leaf.** Tie these 3 together.

2. Add **1/2 tsp. salt,** cover and simmer about 10 minutes, or until tender.

3. Remove the tied spices, drain scallops and reserve the liquid. Cut the scallops into fine pieces and set aside.

4. Sauté **1/2 lb. fresh mushrooms,** chopped, in **4 tablespoons butter,** for about 3 minutes with **1/3 cup minced onion.**

5. Add **1 tablespoon minced parsley, 2 tablespoons water,** and 1 tsp. **fresh lemon juice.** Cover and simmer 5 to 10 minutes.

6. Strain liquid into seasoned wine. Add vegetable mixture to scallops.

7. In another saucepan, blend **1/4 cup butter,** melted, with **1/4 cup flour** until mixture boils.

8. Remove from heat and gradually stir in wine-vegetable liquid. Return to heat and bring to a rapid boil, stirring constantly. Cook 2 minutes.

9. Slightly beat **2 egg yolks,** and **1/4 cup heavy cream.** Remove sauce from heat and gradually add to eggs and cream mixture. Stir in scallop mixture.

10. Fill 8 buttered shells or ramekins, and sprinkle with **1/3 cup [1 slice] dry buttered bread crumbs.** Set shells on baking sheet and bake in 450 degree oven for 10 minutes.

QUICK APPETIZERS

Gefilte fish miniatures (fishlets), are delicious served with **horseradish. Herring in sour cream** or **herring** in **wine sauce** are quick and easy with **rye bread.**

HOT CHILI MUSHROOM FONDUE

1. In top of double boiler, over water, place contents of one can **cream of mushroom soup**, 10 ounces cut up **cheddar cheese** and cook, stirring until smooth and melted.

2. Open and drain a 4 ounce can of roasted, peeled **green chilies**. Remove seeds and cut finely. Stir chilies into cheese and mushroom mixture.

3. Pour into chafing or fondue dish, keep hot. Serve hot with **tortilla chips.**

SMOKED SALMON CORNUCOPIAS

1. Whip **1 cup cream*** and mix with **1/2 jar prepared horseradish**, season with a little fresh **grated pepper.**

2. Place **2 heaping Tbsp.** of this mixture on one end of each salmon slice and roll into a cornucopia shape. If slices are very wide, fold them in half of their width.

3. Slice **2 lemons** to 12 thin rounds and place a salmon cornucopia on each side.

4. Sprinkle a little **chopped parsley** on the open end of each cornucopia and chill well.

*If you desire: Instead of using cream, you may use whipped cream cheese.

CHOPPED HERRING

1. Drain **one large 32 oz. jar of herring** in wine sauce. Place herring and the **onions** in the jar, in meat grinder. Grind with **3 apples** that have been peeled and cored, and **6 hard boiled eggs.**

2. Add a little **white pepper** and a little **sugar** to taste.

3. Remove crusts from **2 slices of light rye bread.** Pour a little **cider vinegar** in a shallow dish, and break up slices of rye bread into small pieces and place in vinegar. Add another slice or two if necessary. When all the vinegar is absorbed, mix this into the herring, onion and egg mixture. Add **2 or 3 Tbls. sweet red wine** and enjoy on rye bread. Chopped herring should be sour but have enough sugar to cut.

SWEET AND SOUR SHRIMP

1. In a bowl place **2 lbs. fresh** or **frozen shrimp** that have been cooked, deveined, and are thoroughly dry.

2. Slice **one large onion** very thin and separate into rings.

3. Make a marinade sauce of (a) **1 pint Miracle Whip Salad Dressing** and (b) **juice of 1/2 lemon.**

4. Mix shrimp, onions and marinade and let stand overnight.

LOX SPREAD

1. Mix the following altogether until it is a loose spreading consistency: **cream cheese,** whipped with **milk, worcestershire sauce, onion juice, cut pieces of lox** (smoked salmon).

2. Slice **miniature bagels** in half and warm.

3. Serve lox spread in bowl with bagels around it and little knives for guests to spread them.

CHEESE AND CAVIAR

1. Beat **one 8 oz. pkg. cream cheese,** with a fork, adding a little **milk** and **onion juice.**

2. When it is of spreading consistency, place in a mound on a serving plate.

3. Place a mound of **black caviar** on top of the cream cheese, Squeeze a little **fresh lemon juice** over caviar. Garnish with **riced hard boiled eggs.**

ANCHOVY RAW VEGETABLE DIP

1. Place an **8 oz. package, very soft cream cheese** in bowl. Add 2 tablespoons **mayonnaise, 1 tablespoon milk.** Mash and blend with a fork. Add **anchovy paste** and fresh **lemon juice** to taste. Sprinkle with **paprika** and blend until it loses its white color. Chop a few **pimento stuffed olives** and stir in.

2. Serve in a small bowl with strips of **zuccini, yellow squash, carrots, celery,** sliced **mushrooms, cauliflowerets, cherry tomatoes,** and **broccoli buds.**

TINY CREAM PUFFS

1. Combine **4 Tbsp. butter** and **1/2 cup water** in saucepan and heat to boiling.

2. Add **1/2 cup flour** and a **dash of salt** and stir vigorously. Cook, stirring constantly, until mixture pulls away from sides of pan and forms a ball that does not separate.

3. Remove from heat, cool slightly.

4. Add **2 eggs** and beat until smooth.

5. Drop batter by scant teaspoonsful, 2 inches apart, on greased cooky sheet.

6. Bake about 400° for 20 minutes or until golden brown. Cool on rack.

7. To serve, cut off tops and fill with chicken salad or seafoods. Makes 4 dozen.

STUFFED MUSHROOMS

1. Wash and drain well, **16 large fresh mushrooms.** Separate stems and cups. Saute in **margarine or butter** with cup side down only. Remove from pan and turn cup side up on plate.

2. Chop mushroom stems. Mince a **garlic clove** and a **small onion.** Saute until browned.

3. Mix **1/2 cup fine dry bread crumbs** in a bowl with **1 large beaten egg, salt** and **pepper.** Add mushroom stems and onions that have been sauted. Mix well together.

4. Fill cups with stuffing. Arrange cups in skillet, with melted butter, dot with butter and sprinkle with **Parmesan cheese.** Place cover on skillet and cook gently until done. If you prefer to bake in oven instead, just place on well buttered baking sheets and bake at 375 degrees, for 15 to 20 minutes. Serve hot.

CHICKEN LIVERS

1. Sauté **chicken livers** in skillet with **margarine.**

2. When thoroughly cooked, **salt** and lightly **pepper.**

3. Serve hot on cocktail picks or in a chafing dish.

HOT CHEESE PUFFS

1. Place one **8 oz. pkg. very soft cream cheese** in a bowl, add a little **milk** and whip until smooth.

2. Add **1 egg yolk, 1 tsp. baking powder, pinch of salt** and a **dash of white pepper.** Blend in until smooth.

3. You may add **grated onion, anchovy paste,** or **spread a little chutney** on. This mixture should be spread on **white melba toast rounds,** then sprinkle with **paprika.** Let mixture set on toast rounds for a while, then toast, just before serving, until puffed and brown. Serve hot.

FILLED GOUDA OR EDAM CHEESE

Hollow a **Gouda** or **Edam cheese** out. Blend a **half pint of cream,** that has been whipped, with **1 tablespoon prepared mustard, Worcestershire sauce,** (or **2Tbsp. beer**) and the **softened cheese** you have scooped out, together. Refill cheese shell and serve with crackers.

CAVIAR MOUSSE

1. Soften **1 tablespoon gelatin** in **1/2 cup cold water.**

2. Add **1/2 cup boiling water** and the **juice of 1/2 a lemon.** Stir until all is dissolved. Cool.

3. Blend **2 cups sour cream** and **3 oz. of very soft cream cheese,** add **1/4 tsp. dry mustard** and mix well together.

4. With a wire whisk, gently blend gelatin and cheese mixtures all together. Chill. When it starts to gel, fold in about **3 oz. black** or **red** (**salmon**) **caviar.** Reserve some for garnish. (Use 3¾ or 4 oz. jars.)

5. Pour into a 2½ cup mold or spoon into small individual molds, 6 or 8 depending on the size. Refrigerate until firm and ready to serve.

6. Serve with **crackers** or **melba toast rounds.** When you unmold to serve, garnish with a tiny bit of **caviar** on top and **watercress.**

Breads

BREADS

Index

CHEESE TORTE WITH KUCHEN DOUGH

Kuchen Dough:

1. In large bowl place **2 1/2 cups flour, 1/2 tsp. salt, 4 Tbsp. butter, 1 egg** (slightly beaten), **3 tsp. baking powder, 1/2 cup sugar** and **1/2 cup milk.**

2. Mix like pie crust and place in 9 inch spring form pan. Moisten edges with cold water to make it stick.

Cheese Filling:

1. In large mixing bowl beat **3 eggs** very well.

2. Add **1 cup sugar, 2 Tbsp.** of melted **butter,** and **1 tsp. vanilla.**

3. Dissolve **1 Tbsp. cornstarch** in **1 cup sour cream.** Add this to above mixture along with a **small 12 oz. box** of **small curd creamed cottage cheese** and mix well.

4. Pour mixture into crust. Sprinkle **sugar and cinnamon mixture** on top.

5. Bake in 375° oven for one hour.

SHORTCAKE

1. Combine **2 cups sifted flour, 4 tsp. baking powder, 1/2 tsp. salt,** and **2 tbsp. sugar.**

2. Work in **1/4 cup butter** with fingers or use pastry blender. Add **3/4 cup milk** gradually.

3. Put on floured board, divide into two parts and roll or pat out one part to fit 9" cake pan, using the least possible flour to roll.

4. Place one part in pan; spread lightly with melted butter. Roll out second part and place on top.

5. Bake 15 minutes in 450° oven.

6. Slice **1 quart fresh strawberries** or **fresh peaches** and sweeten with powdered sugar. Place between layers. Decorate with berries on top in whipped cream. Serve immediately.

FRENCH TOAST

1. Use **day old egg bread,** 2 eggs for 3 slices of bread.

2. Beat **eggs,** with a little **milk.**

3. Dip bread into egg mixture, first on one side, then on the other.

4. In hot **butter** in covered skillet, sauté bread on each side until crisp and golden.

5. Place French toast on plate and lightly sprinkle with **confectioners' sugar.**

6. Serve immediately with syrup.

HOLIDAY TWIST BREAD

1. Scald **3/4 cup milk.** Add **1 stick butter (1/2 cup).** After it melts in milk, add **1/3 cup granulated sugar** and **1/2 tsp. salt.** Cool until lukewarm.

2. Dissolve **1 package** of cake **yeast** in **1/4 cup warm water.**

3. In large bowl place **4 1/2 cups pre-sifted flour** (or sift regular flour), milk mixture, dissolved yeast, **2 eggs, juice of 1/2 lemon,** and mix well.

4. On heavily floured board, knead dough. Sprinkle with **golden raisins** and work in. Knead dough until smooth.

5. Place in very large buttered bowl. Cover with dish towel and let rise for about 1 hour in a warm place until double in size.

6. Punch dough down. Divide in half and place on floured board. Roll each half between hands into 30" rope. Place one rope vertically; lay other one over it horizontally, crossing in the middle. Lift top end of vertical rope down to left side of its bottom end. Lift left end of horizontal rope up and over lower two ropes. Repeat this with right end of same rope. Braid 4 ropes together to end and pinch ends together. Place on large greased cookie sheet.

7. Brush with mixture of **1 small beaten egg,** diluted with a little **water**.

8. Let rise in covered warm place until almost double in size.

9. Bake at 325 ° for 10 minutes, then turn oven to 350° and bake for 30 to 35 minutes.

10. Remove from cookie sheet and cool on rack.

LEMON COFFEE BREAD

1. Cream **2 sticks soft butter** with **2 cups sugar.**

2. Drop in **3 eggs plus 2 yolks** and beat very well.

3. Add 1 cup sour cream, juice of 1 lemon, grated rind of 2 lemons, 1/4 tsp. almond extract, 4 cups sifted flour, 1/2 tsp. salt, 1/2 tsp. soda, 1 Tbsp. baking powder. Mix gently until smooth.

4. Fold in **2 stiffly beaten egg whites.**

5. Stir in 3/4 cup golden raisins and 3/4 cup chopped nuts.

6. Pour into buttered tube pan. Bake at 350° for one hour. Cool on cake rack.

7. Before serving, make a glaze of 1 heaping **Tbsp. butter, 1 1/4 cup confectioners' sugar, juice and rind of one lemon.** Beat well together and spread over top of cake.

CROISSANTS

1. Cream **1 stick very soft butter, 2 eggs, 3 Tablespoons sugar, 1 teaspoon salt, and 1 cup sour cream** together.

2. Add **3 cups sifted flour** that has **1 package (1/4 oz.) dry yeast** added to it. Add **1/4 cup lukewarm water.** (If you use cake yeast soften in the lukewarm water for 5 minutes). Beat well in electric mixer.

3. Place in large bowl and knead, adding flour continuously while you knead, until it is smooth and does not stick.

4. Roll out on a lightly floured board, after you divide into three parts. Leave remaining two parts in bowl covered until ready to roll out. Roll into a circle.

5. Heat **2 tablespoons butter,** when melted pour on rolled piece. Spread. For schnecken, mix **sugar** and a little **cinnamon** in a bowl and sprinkle over the butter. Sprinkle on a few **white raisins.**

6. Cut in half, then in fourths, then eighths, until you have sixteen triangle shaped pieces. Then roll starting at the widest part to the narrowest and place on a buttered cookie sheet. Cover with a clean cloth and place in a warm place away from drafts for one hour. Do the same for the other two parts that are remaining in bowl.

7. Bake 375 degrees for 15 to 20 minutes. Brush top with 1 beaten egg white before baking. Makes 4 dozen.

ORANGE BUTTERMILK MUFFINS

1. In large mixing bowl place **2 cups sifted flour,** add **2 teaspoons baking powder, 1/2 teaspoon baking soda,** and **1/3 cup sugar.** Give one stir and make well in center.

2. Mix together **1/3 cup orange juice, 2/3 cup buttermilk, 1/3 cup melted butter** or **margarine** and **1 large beaten egg.** Pour into dry ingredients, add **1/3 cup white raisins.** Stir only until dry ingredients are moistened.

3. Place 12 paper cups in muffin tins and fill 2/3 full. Bake 400° for 20-25 minutes. Serve hot with sweet butter.

PIZZA

1. Put **4 cups sifted flour** in large bowl. Mix **1 package yeast** in **1 and 1/3 cups very warm water** (85 degrees), when dissolved add **1 tsp. salt.** Make a well in the center of the flour and pour this yeast mix in. Pour in **2 tablespoons salad oil.**

2. Mix well together and then knead until there is no loose flour left. About 10 minutes. Knead into a mound. Dust flour over top and then cover with towel. Let rise for about 2 hours. Knead again. Pinch off dough and roll, then pat and stretch dough into pizza pans, two 12" pizza pans that have been lightly greased.

Sauce:

1. Mix well, **1 pkg. French's Pizza sauce mix, 1 can large tomato sauce,** and **1 cup water.** Spread over pizzas. Sprinkle generously with equal amounts of grated **Monterey Jack** and **Mozarella cheese.**

2. Cover with what ever you desire, such as **anchovies, chopped black olive, mushrooms, sausage slices,** lightly **sauteed onions,** etc.

3. Sprinkle with **Romano** and **Parmesan cheese.**

4. Bake 500° for 15 to 20 minutes. Cut while hot with pizza cutter.

BAGELS

1. Dissolve **1 envelope dry yeast** in **1/4 cup lukewarm water.**

2. Scald **1 cup milk.**

3. Dissolve **1/4 cup butter, 1 Tbsp. sugar,** and **1 tsp. salt** in the milk. Cool until it is lukewarm.

4. Add yeast.

5. Place **2 cups flour** in the mixing bowl; make a well in the center and pour in milk mixture. Add **one well beaten egg white.** Mix well, then add gradually a little **under 2 more cups of flour** to make soft dough.

6. Knead dough until smooth and then place in well greased large bowl. Grease top of dough and cover bowl with cloth. Set in warm place (not hot) for about 1 hour or until it rises to double in bulk.

7. Knead again on floured board. Divide dough into quarters. Roll each into long strips. Cut into pieces the size you want your bagel. Shape into rings and pinch ends together. Let stand on board for about 10 minutes or until bagels just begin to rise.

8. Drop bagels into pan of hot water just under the boiling point. Cook on one side and then on the other side.

9. Place them on a greased cookie sheet.

10. Beat **1 egg yolk** with **1 Tbsp. of water** and brush this on top of each bagel. Sprinkle lightly with **poppy seeds.**

11. Bake at 425° until golden brown (15 to 25 minutes) or you may bake at 400° for about 30 minutes.

FRENCH CHEESE & TOMATO SANDWICH

1. Slice and peel **one tomato**. Take **4 slices of white bread** and cut off crusts.

2. **Butter** one side of **each slice of bread**. Place a slice of **Swiss cheese** on two of the bread slices and then the tomato slices over cheese. Place other slice of bread on top.

3. In a pie pan place **3 eggs**, a small amount of **milk** and beat until blended. Add a little **salt**.

4. Place sandwich in mixture, first on one side, then on the other, until bread soaks up egg mixture and is completely coated, even on all sides. Do this to both sandwiches.

5. In large skillet melt **butter,** enough to cover the pan, and place sandwiches in, after a few minutes, turn and cover. Cook on a very low heat. When golden brown, turn over, and cook covered on the other side too until golden brown. Serve hot.

6. You may add a little anchovy paste to the butter if desired.

BLUEBERRY COFFEE CAKE

1. Cream **1 stick butter, 1 cup sugar** and **3 eggs** together.

2. Add **2 cups sifted flour, 1 tsp. baking soda, dash of mace, 1 tsp. baking powder, 1/2 tsp. salt** and **12 ounces of sour cream**. Beat slowly.

3. Add **1/2 tsp. almond extract** and **1 tsp. vanilla**. Beat gently until smooth. Stir in **2 cups fresh blueberries.**

4. Pour 2/3 batter into buttered loaf cake pan 14x10''. Sprinkle **1/2 cup brown sugar** over this and **1/2 cup crushed pecans**. Spread the remaining batter over this, gently so that all of the brown sugar is covered. Bake 50 minutes at 325°.

HONEY BRAN MUFFINS

1. In large bowl place **2 1/2 cups Bran Flakes cereal**. Pour **1 1/4 cups milk** over it and stir. Add **1 egg, 1/2 cup honey, 1/3 cup melted butter (or margarine)** and **1 tablespoon light molasses**. Mix very well.

2. Add **1/2 cup raisins, 1 1/4 cups flour,** and **3 teaspoons baking powder**. Stir only until flour can not be seen.

3. Spoon into greased or lined 2 1/2 inch muffin tins. Makes 12. Bake 400° for 25 minutes.

CINNAMON ROLLS

1. Dissolve **3 pkgs. of yeast** and **4 Tbsp. sugar** in a **quart of milk** that has been scalded and cooled.

2. Add **6 1/2 cups flour** to make sponge. Beat until smooth in electric mixer. Cover with a clean towel and let rise until light in warm place for one hour.

3. In mixing bowl beat **1 cup butter** and **1 1/3 cups sugar**. Add **4 slightly beaten eggs** and beat well.

4. Add **1 cup raisins, 1 tsp. salt** and **6 1/2 cups of flour** again.

5. Knead flour into sponge. Grease hands and knead well until dough does not stick to your hands. Add up to **2 more cups of flour** if necessary.

6. Cover with towel again and set aside in warm place until it doubles in bulk. Divide dough; Dough rolled is approx. 9 x 12 x ¼" thick. Roll 12" side. Cut in 1/2" slices with very sharp knife.

7. Roll out and spread lightly with **butter.** Then sprinkle with **sugar and cinnamon.** Roll as for jelly roll and slice. Roll in sugar and cinnamon mixture.

8. Place in greased pans 1/2 inch apart and let rise again until double in size.

9. Bake at 375° 20 to 30 minutes.

10. This is a large recipe, but you may also make it into rings and use as coffee cakes.

11. Roll enough dough for a round cake pan. Butter dough and cover with sliced apples overlapping. Sprinkle on sugar & cinnamon and cover with sour cream & more sugar and cinnamon. Bake as above. Elegant!

SAVARIN

1. Soften 1 pkg. yeast in ¼ cup warm water.

2. Scald 1/2 cup milk. Drop in 1/3 cup butter and stir until it melts. Cool to lukewarm. Stir in 1/2 cup flour, 1/2 tsp. salt. Beat in 1 egg and the yeast. Add 1 1/2 cups flour. Beat vigorously for 6 or 7 minutes.

3. Cover and let rise in a warm place until double in size (about 1 hour and 15 minutes).

4. Stir down batter and spoon into well greased 6 cup ring mold. Cover and let rise until double (about 45 minutes).

5. Bake 350° for 35 minutes or until top is browned.

6. Cool 5 minutes and remove from mold.

7. Prick top of Savarin in several places with toothpick and slowly drizzle with hot **Savarin syrup.**

8. Let stand for 30 minutes. Baste frequently so that it will soak well.

9. Brush entire surface with warm **Apricot Glaze.**

10. Garnish with **orange slices** and **candied cherries.** Fill center with **2 cups whipping cream** with **2 Tbsp. powdered sugar** and **2 tsp. vanilla** mixed in.

Savarin Syrup:

1. Combine **2 cups sugar** and 1 1/2 cups water and bring to a boil and simmer for 10 min.

2. Remove from heat. Add 1/2 cup rum, a **dozen maraschino cherries.** Pour **3 Tbsp. light corn syrup** over them and heat to boiling. Remove fruit to wax paper and cut orange slices in half. Cool.

Apricot Glaze:

Heat a 12 ounce jar apricot preserves [1 1/4 cups] and stir. Then force through sieve.

PEACHES 'N' CREAM COFFEE CAKE

1. Mix together 1/2 cup sugar, 2 tsp. cinnamon and 1/2 cup chopped pecans. Set aside.

2. In a large mixing bowl, cream together 1 stick butter, 1 cup sugar and 3 eggs. Beat well.

3. Add 2 cups sifted all purpose flour, 1 tsp. baking powder, 1 tsp. baking soda, 1/2 tsp. salt, one cup sour cream and 1 tsp. vanilla. Mix well.

4. Lighlty butter an angel food cake pan.

5. Pour half of batter into pan and slice a fresh peach (or apple) or use sliced frozen or canned peaches, and lay evenly over layer. Sprinkle 3/4 of nut mixture over this.

6. Pour remaining coffee cake batter over this, and then sprinkle remaining nut mixture on top.

7. Bake at 375° for 40 minutes or untill done. Then cool on cake rack for 30 minutes.

8. Remove and serve when you desire.

BREAKFAST SAPPHIRE COFFEE CAKE

1. Sift 2 cups all-purpose flour into bowl. Add 3 tsp. baking powder, 1 tsp. salt and 1/4 cup sugar.

2. With pastry blender, cut 1/4 cup soft butter into dry ingredients until consistency of coarse cornmeal.

3. Make a well in center of flour mixture, and pour in 1/2 cup milk, then drop in 1 whole egg. Stir with fork until all ingredients are moistened and combined.

4. Spread batter evenly in 9 by 1 1/2" round layer cake pan, lightly greased.

5. Arrange 1 1/2 cups drained blueberries over surface of batter, leaving an inch around pan's edge.

6. Sprinkle evenly over top this streusel topping: Mix together 1/2 cup graham cracker crumbs, 1/4 cup butter, 2 Tbsp. sugar, 1/2 tsp. cinnamon.

7. Bake at 400° for 30 minutes. Cool on wire rack. Serve warm with whipped butter.

COFFEE CAKE

1. Cream together **1 cup butter, 2 cups sugar;** add **3 eggs** and beat well.

2. Add **3 1/2 cups sifted cake flour, 4 tsp. baking powder, 1/2 tsp. salt, 1 large can evaporated milk, 1 tsp. vanilla** and **1/2 tsp. almond extract.**

3. When this is all mixed well together, pour into well buttered and floured angel food cake pan or bundt pan. Pour only half of batter into pan.

4. Make filling of **3 tsp. cinnamon, 1/4 cup sugar, 1/2 cup of chopped pecans** and **2 Tbsp. of melted butter.**

5. Sprinkle half of filling mixture in cake, then add the remaining half of batter and sprinkle remainder of filling mixture on top of cake.

6. Bake at 350° for 1 hour or until done.

SOUR CREAM COFFEE CAKE

1. Cream **1 stick butter** and **1 cup sugar** together well. Add **2 slightly beaten eggs.** Beat until smooth.

2. Add **1 tsp. baking soda** to **1 cup of sour cream,** and beat into creamed mixture.

3. Add **2 cups sifted flour, 1 tsp. baking powder, 1 tsp. vanilla,** and **1 Tbsp. apricot sour or brandy.**

4. Make a topping of **1/4 cup sugar, 1 tsp. cinnamon,** and **2 tsp. chopped nuts.** Set aside.

5. Add 1/2 of topping mixture to cake batter and grate in **1/2 square of bittersweet chocolate.**

6. Pour into 9 inch greased tube pan.

7. Sprinkle remainder of topping over cake.

8. Bake at 325°. Turn off oven after cake has baked for 40 minutes and open door and allow cake to cool in oven for less than an hour.

PARTY SANDWICH LOAF CAKE

1. Trim all crusts from **day-old loaf** of **unsliced white bread.**

2. Lay loaf on side and slice it lengthwise into 5 even slices 1/2" thick. Lightly **butter** before spreading slices.

3. Spread bottom slice with **cheese spread** (two 5 oz. **jars sharp cheese** blended with **2 Tbsp. hot water).**

4. Spread second slice with **tuna salad.**

5. Place bread slice with tuna salad on top of slice spread with cheese.

6. Spread **egg salad** on third slice and place on top of previous layer.

7. Spread fourth layer with **salmon salad** and place on top of egg salad slice.

8. Top loaf with last slice of bread. Be sure all sides are even and remove any oozing filling.

9. Frost top and sides with **"frosting"** (12 oz. cream cheese thinned to spreading consistency with **milk**, about **1/2 cup** milk). You may tint with food coloring.

10. Refrigerate loaf for several hours; if chilled overnight, cover with box. Garnish.

11. Makes ten 1" slices.

IRISH OATMEAL BREAD

1. Place in a large bowl **3 cups sifted all-purpose flour, 1 1/4 cups quick rolled oats, 1 1/2 Tbsp. baking powder** and **1 tsp. salt.**

2. In another bowl beat **1 egg, 1/4 cup honey** and **1 1/2 cups milk**, and mix well.

3. Pour egg mixture into oat mixture, and stir just until dry ingredients are moistened—it will not be smooth.

4. Spread batter into 9 1/2 x 5 1/4 x 2 1/4" loaf pan. Bake 1 hour, 15 minutes at 350°

5. Turn loaf out of pan on rack. While still warm, brush top with **1 Tbsp. melted butter.**

BANANA BREAD

1. Cream together 1/2 cup butter and 1 cup sugar.

2. Add 2 eggs and beat well.

3. Mash 3 large or 4 small ripe bananas with a fork and beat into above mixture.

4. Add 3 Tbsp. sour cream, pinch of salt, 1 tsp. baking soda and 2 cups flour and beat until smooth.

5. Mix in 1 cup chopped walnuts.

6. Bake at 350° for 1 hour in one pound coffee cans well greased or small loaf bread pans.

TEA SANDWICHES
Bread Cups

1. Cut 1 loaf whole wheat bread or white bread into slices 1 inch thick.

2. Cut bread into rounds with biscuit cutter.

3. With kitchen shears hollow out rounds leaving 1/4 inch sides and bottoms.

4. To serve, brush butter inside each bread cup. Fill with egg salad and garnish with slices of ripe olives or make into toast cups by placing buttered cups in muffin tins. Bake in 350° oven until crisp. Fill with hot crab mixture or other filling. Makes 30.

Pinwheels

1. Cut 1 loaf unsliced white bread into lengthwise slices about 1/4 inch thick.

2. Spread 4 slices bread with soft margarine. Then spread chicken salad (very fine) made with breast of chicken, mayonnaise, mashed pimento on each slice using about 3 Tbsp. of chicken salad.

3. Trim crusts. Roll up, beginning at narrow end.

4. Wrap in plastic wrap and then foil. Chill. Slice into 3/8 inch pinwheels. (This makes 20. To use whole loaf, double recipe.)

Finger Sandwiches

1. Spread 20 thin slices of raisin bread with soft butter. Spread half of the slices with cream cheese and olives, or tuna salad.

2. Top with remaining bread. Trim crusts. Cut sandwiches into 3 inch fingers. Wrap and refrigerate. Makes 30.

Fruits and Molds

FRUITS AND MOLDS

Index

ORANGE MOLD

1. Place **one 6 oz. pkg. orange-pineapple flavored gelatin** in a bowl.

2. Pour **1 1/2 cups boiling water** over it and stir to dissolve.

3. Stir in **1 1/3 cups lemon-flavored sparkling water** and stir to blend. Chill until gelatin mounds when dropped from a spoon.

4. Pour 2 cups of gelatin mixture into souffle dish. Leave remainder of mixture in bowl at room temperature.

5. In gelatin mixture in souffle dish, arrange **5 slices of peaches** into a design and **1/3 cup seedless green grapes** (or you may use 1/3 cup drained pineapple chunks instead of grapes.

6. Carefully spoon remaining gelatin mixture over this fruit and make the top smooth and level. Refrigerate until almost firm, about 40 minutes.

7. Beat softened **1 8-oz. pkg.** and **1 3-oz. pkg. cream cheese** with fork. Beat in **6 Tbsp. milk**, dash of **cinnamon**, **1/4 tsp. nutmeg** and **1/3 cup finely crushed pecans**. Beat until smooth.

8. Spoon this cheese and nut mixture over gelatin — make it very even. Refrigerate.

9. Now make up another **6 oz. pkg.** of **orange-pineapple flavored gelatin**. Dissolve in **1 1/3 cups boiling water**. Stir in **1 1/3 cup** either **pineapple juice or lemon flavored sparkling water**.

10. Refrigerate until it mounds when dropped from spoon and carefully spoon over cream cheese and refrigerate until next day when ready to serve.

11. Before serving, place souffle bowl in to pan of hot water up to 1/3 inch of its top for 1 or 2 minutes. Remove and run long spatula around edge and be sure it goes to bottom of dish.

12. Invert and center serving plate on top of souffle dish, invert both and shake gently until gelatin slips out.

13. Garnish with bunches of seedless green grapes.

APRICOT MARSHMALLOW MOLD

1. Dissolve **one 6 oz. pkg. Apricot gelatin in 3 cups boiling water.** Add **2 six oz. cans frozen orange juice.** Stir until melted.

2. Refrigerate until slightly thickened.

3. Add **2 cups marshmallow creme** (1 pint jar) and beat with electric beater until smooth.

4. Pour into 2 quart mold and chill until firm.

5. Unmold and serve.

APRICOT RING

1. Drain **1 cup** (9 oz. can) **crushed pineapple,** (save syrup).

2. Soften **2 enelopes unflavored gelatin** in 1/4 **cup cold water** and the **reserved juice** from the pineapple.

3. Heat **1 1/2 cups apricot nectar** to the boiling point and add to gelatin. Stir until gelatin is dissolved. Add **1/4 cup lemon juice** and cool to room temperature.

4. Very slowly, carefully pouring down side of bowl, add **1 cup lemon-lime carbonated bevarage,** very well chilled. Stir very gently with up and down motion.

5. Chill until partially set. Add crushed pineapple stirring gently up and down again.

6. Fill a 5 1/2 cup ring mold 1/3 full, chill until almost firm.

7. Blend **one 3 oz. pkg.** of **cream cheese** that is softened, **3 Tbsp. mayonnaise;** stir in **1/3 cup chopped celery** and **1/4 cup chopped pecans.** Spoon this over layer of almost firm gelatin and spread evenly.

8. Add remaining gelatin and chill. Serves 10.

STUFFED APRICOT MOLD

1. Make **one large size package of orange jello,** and **one large size package orange-lemon jello,** according to directions and pour into a large ring mold.

2. Whip **one soft package of cream cheese [3 oz.].** Add **crushed walnuts** or **pecans.** Place a small amount in the center of **whole, peeled, apricots,** after you remove the seeds. Arrange in mold with **pineapple chunks, pear halves,** and **maraschino cherries.**

CRUNCHY CRANBERRY MOLD

1. Drain **syrup** from 1 #2 can [20 ozs.] of **crushed pineapple** and add enough **water** to make 1 1/2 cups liquid. Heat to boiling and pour over **2 packages of lemon flavored gelatin** in bowl. Stir until completely dissolved.

2. Stir in crushed pineapple and 1/2 cup lemon juice, 3 Tbsp. orange peel (chopped or shredded) **3 cups whole cranberry sauce** (canned or fresh) and **1/3 cup chopped walnuts.**

3. Pour into 8 inch ring mold. Chill until firm.

4. Dip mold in hot water for 15 seconds. Invert over serving plate to unmold.

HOT FRUIT COMPOTE

1. Melt **4 tablespoons butter** or **margarine** in skillet. Add **1/4 cup brown sugar, 2 tablespoons cornstarch, 1/2 cup sherry,** and **3/4 cup apricot sour** or **brandy.**

2. Drain **juice from large size cans** of **peach halves, pear halves, apricot (peeled) halves** and **pineapple rings.** Slice pineapple rings in half. Mix juice together and add half to skillet. Cook gently. Place fruit halves plus **pitted prunes** and **bing cherries,** in hot mixture in skillet. Cook for a few minutes, then lift fruit out and arrange in large flat oven proof casserole. Pour syrup over this.

3. Bake at 425 degrees for 35 to 45 minutes. Pour into chafing dish and serve hot.

ORANGE-GLAZED PEARS

1. Thoroughly drain a **29 oz. can of pear halves.**

2. Combine **2 Tblsp. apricot preserves** and **1 cup orange juice** in skillet. Heat to boiling, stirring constantly. Reduce heat.

3. Place pears, cut side down, in skillet. Simmer and baste often until they are glazed.

4. Arrange pear halves in shallow serving dish, spoon glaze over them. Chill at least an hour.

5. Place two halves of pears together. Garnish with **sprig of mint** on top.

HEAVENLY PEACH SALAD

1. Drain a **29 oz. can of peach halves**, reserving **1/2 cup of the juice.**

2. Cut all but two of the halves into small pieces.

3. Cut the two halves into thick slices. If you use fresh peaches, you will need about 4 medium size.

4. Soften **1 pkg. gelatin** in **3 Tbsp. cold water.** Then dissolve in hot peach juice. Cool.

5. Blend into one very soft **8 oz. pkg. cream cheese, 1 1/2 Tbsp. lemon juice** and **1/2 cup mayonnaise.**

6. Add cut up peaches to cream cheese-mayonnaise mixture. Blend in cooled gelatin mixture and fold in **1/2 cup whipped cream.**

7. If you want a white mold, leave it this way. If you desire a pale pink mold, before you fold in whipped cream, stir in a little **maraschino cherry juice.**

8. Pour into 4 individual molds and chill until firm.

9. Garnish with maraschino cherries and peach slices.

CINNAMON APPLE SALAD

1. Core and peel **4 or 5 apples** and let them cook in the following syrup: **1 cup water, 1/2 cup sugar, a few drops of red food coloring, red hots (candy)** and **cinnamon stick.** Keep turning and cooking apples until they are bright red and done.

2. Thin **one small pkg.** of **cream cheese** with a little milk. Place apples on lettuce leaf. Fill centers with cream cheese mixture. Pour remaining syrup over outside of apples. Chill and serve.

CANTALOUPE RINGS

1. Remove peeling from **cantaloupe.** Slice cantaloupe into rings and remove seeds. Place on plate.

2. Scoop **a ball of ice cream** into center of ring. Top with a small sugar cooky standing up.

JELLIED PINEAPPLE SLICES

1. Make **lime gelatin** with half the water called for in package directions.

2. Pour liquid off **20 oz. can of sliced pineapple** and replace with lime gelatin.

3. Chill until set.

4. Run a little hot water on can's sides and bottom. Cut bottom from can and use to push mold out.

5. Slice between pineapple slices and serve.

PINEAPPLE SOUR CREAM SALAD

1. Dissolve **1 package [small] lemon gelatin in 1 cup hot water.**

2. Add **1/4 cup cold water, 2 Tbsp. lemon juice** and **1 cup sour cream.**

3. Beat until blended. Chill to thicken slightly.

4. Set in ice and water; whip until thick and foamy.

5. Fold in **1 1/2 cups drained, crushed pineapple.** Chill. Unmold. Serves 6-8.

FRESH PINEAPPLE IN HOT RUM

1. Slice **2 large pineapples** into 8 slices and place in large flat pan.

2. Sprinkle with granulated sugar.

3. When sugar is absorbed, drop slices with **1 cup light rum** into plastic bag and place in bowl. Marinate for several hours, turning occasionally.

4. Meanwhile, make a sauce: (a) Melt **1 stick butter** in double boiler; stir in rum in which pineapple was marinated. (b) Add **4 well beaten egg yolks.** (c) Cook in double boiler and stir constantly just unil sauce thickens.

5. To serve, drain pineapple slices. Place on dessert plate and spoon sauce over them.

CUCUMBER RING MOLD

1. Dissolve **2 small pkgs. lime flavored gelatin** in **1 1/2 cups hot water;** add **one 3 oz. pkg. and one 8 oz. pkg. of softened cream cheese, 2 cups mayonnaise, 2 tsp. prepared horseradish, and 1/4 tsp. salt.**

2. Beat in mixer until smooth. Add **4 Tbsp. fresh lemon juice.**

3. Chill until partially set.

4. Stir in **1/4 cup** finely sliced **green onions** and **1 1/2 cups drained, shredded unpared cucumber.** Line large mold with very thinly sliced unpared cucumbers.

5. Turn mixture into mold and chill until set.

6. Unmold to serve and fill center with crabmeat, lobster, tuna or salmon and garnish with lemon and hard boiled egg slices.

PERFECTION SALAD

1. **Thoroughly mix 2 envelopes unflavored gelatin, 1/2 cup sugar, and 1 tsp. salt. Dissolve gelatin in 1 1/2 cups boiling water. Then add 1 1/2 cups cold water, 1/2 cup vinegar and 2 Tbsp. lemon juice.**

2. Add **2 cups finely shredded cabbage.** Add **1 cup finely chopped celery, 1/2 cup chopped green pepper, 1/4 cup diced pimento and 1/3 cup stuffed green olives slices.**

3. Pour into Pyrex loaf pan 8½" x 4½" x 2½". Chill until firm.

4. Unmold and garnish with carrot curls and ripe olives.

GINGER WHIP

1. Dissolve **one large package orange flavored gelatin and one small package lemon gelatin** into **3 cups hot water.** Add 2 1/2 cups ginger ale and 1/2 cup pineapple juice.

2. Chill until slightly thickened.

3. Add **one 20 oz. can (drained) pineapple chunks, a small can (drained) mandarin oranges** and some **maraschino cherries.**

4. Turn into 2 quart ring mold and chill until firm.

5. Unmold and serve. Garnish with thin slices of oranges and mint leaves. Serves around 14.

STRAWBERRY PRESERVES

1. Wash **3 heaping tea cups** of **fresh strawberries** and pour into kettle.

2. Pour **3 level tea cups** of **sugar** over them.

3. Start cooking very slowly and when sugar is dissolved, turn up burner to high. When it starts to boil, time for about ten minutes or until thick when you put a little on a saucer and place in freezer and it does not run. Never touch spoon to kettle's bottom. Skim often.

4. Remove from stove and pour in loaf cake pans.

5. Make 2 or 3 more batches, using the same method, and pour on top of first batch. Stir in a little fresh lemon juice.

6. Let stand overnight.

7. Next day, pour into sterilized jars and let stand some more. You may even wait an extra day. Pour paraffin over to seal.

CRANBERRY JELLY

1. Wash and pick over **1 quart fresh cranberries** (or four cups).

2. Boil **2 cups water** and **2 cups sugar** to a syrup for 10 minutes.

3. Add cranberries. Cover first and when it starts to boil hard, uncover and cook well until cranberries are clear. Strain through food mill.

4. Pour into mold and chill. You may add **diced celery** and **crushed walnuts** if you desire.

5. When cold, unmold and serve.

MAYONNAISE

1. Beat **3 egg yolks** until thick and lemon colored. Using oil dripper on your mixer, let **1 1/2 to 2 cups of oil** drip in slowly and beat slowly. The mayonnaise should be stiff enough to hold its shape.

2. When only half of the oil has dripped into mixture, add **1 tsp. sugar,** 1/2 tsp. salt, 1/2 tsp dry mustard and **3 Tbsp. lemon juice.**

3. When oil is finished dripping, beat two minutes longer.

4. Refrigerate.

THOUSAND ISLAND DRESSING

1. Blend these ingredients together: **2 cups mayonnaise, 1/2 cup chili sauce,** and **3/4 cup sweet pickle relish.**

2. Whip **1/2 cup cream** and blend all together.

ANCHOVY SALAD DRESSING

1. Chop **1 can anchovies, 2 green onions, 1/2 cup parsley, 1 clove garlic** squeeze in garlic press. Chop until it is almost a paste.

2. Add **2 heaping Tbsp. anchovy paste.** Stir in **1 1/4 cup mayonnaise** and squeeze in **fresh lemon juice** to thin.

POPPY SEED DRESSING for Fruit Salad

1. Combine **1/2 cup sugar, 1 tsp. dry mustard, 1/4 cup cider vinegar, 1 tsp. salt** in a mixing bowl.

2. Gradually beat in **1 cup salad oil.** Beat until thick and smooth.

3. Stir in **1 1/2 Tbsp. poppy seeds.** Stir in **1/4 cup orange marmalade.**

FRENCH DRESSING

1. Mix together in very large measuring cup: **1 cup catsup, 3/4 cup sugar, 1 cup salad oil, 1 cup salad vinegar, 1/2 tsp. dry mustard, a dash of Worcestershire sauce, black pepper,** and **1 clove garlic** (pressed if desired).

2. Pour into bottle and shake vigorously. Refrigerate.

OIL and VINEGAR DRESSING

1. Mix together **2/3 cup salad oil, 1/4 cup salad vinegar.** Shake in a little **celery salt, lemon pepper, paprika** and a little **dry mustard.**

2. Squeeze **1 or 2 cloves of fresh garlic** through a garlic press, and juice of **one lemon.** Pour into bottle and shake vigorously. When the dressing is on the salad, you may add crumbled **blue cheese.** Substitute **taragon vinegar** and add **snipped fresh dill** for variety.

BRANDIED FRUIT

How to prepare a "start" for brandied fruit. Once you "start" the fruit, you simply add more to keep it going. WORTHY has a yeast that is responsible for fermentation. VINTAGE CUP is "started" with brandy or rum and the alcohol is replaced at the same time as the fruit. The flavor varies each time something is added. These are fun to "start" and give for gifts.

WORTHY

1. Place **3/4 cup drained crushed pineapple, 3/4 cup chopped peaches, 8 maraschino cherries, cut in half, 1 1/2 cups sugar** and **1 tbsp. dry yeast**, in a one quart container with loose fitting top. Stir 3 times a day. After two weeks add:

2. **1 cup crushed pineapple** and **1 cup sugar**. Stir every 2 days.

3. At the end of two weeks again add **1 cup chopped peaches**, and **1 cup sugar**. Stir again every 2 days.

4. At the end of two more weeks add **1 cup maraschino cherries**, cut in half.

5. Stir every two or three days and let it "work": for at least two weeks. To keep "starter" going, add more fruit and sugar every two weeks. At the end of the eighth week, add fruit and sugar in the above order and amounts every two weeks as written. To do this, you will have to divide the "starter" into two jars, or you can use a larger jar to begin with. Do not let "starter" go below three cups.

VINTAGE CUP

1. The canned fruits may be **pineapple, cherries, sliced peaches** or **apricots.** Dried fruits which include **figs, prunes, apricots, dates, raisins,** etc.. You may also use preserved fruits: **brandied** or **candied,** or **fruit jam** or **preserves.**

2. Add **bitters, whole cloves** and a dash of **cinnamon.**

3. Use **brandy** or **rum** to cover. To keep indefinitely, replenish at will, but always add enough spirits, including cordials to cover. Some people add just a cup of fruit and a cup of sugar each every two weeks and no more alcohol.

PLUM PRESERVES

1. Wash and drain **plums,** remove seeds. Pack full into a measuring cup. For each cup of plums use **3/4 cup sugar.** Place all in a large kettle, add a little **orange juice** and squeeze in **1/4 of a lemon.** Stir and cook slowly.

2. Stir occasionally, turning heat up slightly and simmer close to an hour or until it is cooked down.

3. Remove from heat and cool. When cold, pour into sterilized jars. I use this for my SOUR CREAM TORTE filling.

RASPBERRY SAUCE

1. Wash and pick over **fresh raspberries.** Measure **4 cups.** Put through a food mill or sieve and strain.

2. Place **2 cups granulated sugar** and **1 cup water** in saucepan. Stir until it comes to a boil.

3. Cook until 220° on candy thermometer. Add strained raspberries and again bring to 220°. Skim until clear.

4. Pour into sterilized jar. Makes 1 pint.

APRICOT JAM

1. Wash and stone **6 to 8 large apricots.** Cut into eighths. Weigh apricots and place in saucepan. Cover with equal weight of **sugar.** Cover and let stand 12 hours.

2. Cook gently until thick, about 40 minutes or longer. Squeeze in **fresh lemon juice.**

3. Pour into sterilized jar. Makes 1 pint. Excellent to brush on cakes and pastries, or use in strudel filling.

Vegetables and Cheeses

VEGETABLES AND CHEESES

Index

VEGETABLES AND CHEESES

GREEN BEANS ALMOND

1. Cook frozen, **french cut green beans** as package directs, and drain when cooked.

2. Cook **slivered blanched almonds** (or whole) in **butter** over low heat, stirring occasionally, until golden brown. Remove from heat.

3. Pour hot over beans.

GREEN BEANS AND MUSHROOM CASSEROLE

1. In a large skillet melt **1 stick margarine**, add **1 diced onion** and **3/4 lb fresh mushrooms**, washed and sliced in half. Brown over medium heat.

2. In a small bowl place **2 heaping Tbsp. cornstarch**. Gradually stir in **1 cup milk**. Pour this into **onions and mushrooms**, and turn heat lower and stir.

3. Add **2 cans [16 ozs. each] one of French cut green beans** and one of **kitchen cut green beans**. Stir well.

4. Add **4 ozs. of diced pimentoes** and a large wedge of **cheddar cheese** cut up. Add more **cheese** and another **cup of milk**. Stir in a little **soy sauce**.

5. Pour into large casserole and bake at 325 degrees for 35-45 minutes. If you desire you may sprinkle a can of **French fried onion rings** over casserole. Serve hot. Serves 8-10 people.

BAKED ACORN SQUASH

1. Cut **squash** in half lengthwise.

2. Fill a long shallow pan about 1/4 full with **water**. Place 2 squash, cut side down, in pan and bake at 350° for about 30 minutes.

3. Turn squash over and in cavity of each, place a large lump of **butter** and **brown sugar**. Add sherry, if desired.

4. Bake until tender. Serve immediately.

FRENCH FRIED ONION RINGS

1. Place **1 cup flour** and **1/4 tsp. salt** in bowl.

2. Slightly beat **1 egg**, add **1 cup milk** and **1 Tbsp. salad oil**. Beat until smooth, gradually adding flour.

3. Dip onion rings into batter.

4. Fry in deep hot fat(375°) 2 to 5 minutes.

5. This makes 1 1/4 cups batter, enough for 30 onion rings.

TOMATO SOUFFLÉ

1. Cut 1 inch slice from the tops of **4 large**, firm **tomatoes** and scoop out pulp. Save pulp and set tomato shells to drain (save any juice).

2. Simmer pulp and juice with **2 cloves, 1 tsp. onion flakes** (or grated onion) and add a **pinch of basil.** Cook until it reduces to a cup.

3. Strain and mash (or put through sieve) just so you get everything but the seeds.

4. Melt **1 heaping Tbsp. butter** and stir in **1 Tbsp. flour** and **1 tsp. instant potatoes**; add **1/2 cup hot milk.** Cook and stir until thick and smooth.

5. Beat **2 egg yolks** until light in color.

6. Very slowly pour hot cream sauce into egg yolks, beating well. Add the tomato puree; add a dash of **salt** and **pepper** and **1/2 tsp. cognac** (or sherry). Cool.

7. About 40 minutes before serving, beat **2 egg whites** stiff but not dry. Stir 1/4 of whites into sauce and then pour the sauce over the rest of the whites, folding in lightly.

8. Cut tiny slice from bottom of each tomato and stand them upright in shallow pan.

9. Fill tomatoes 3/4 full.

10. Bake at 375° (preheated oven) for 30 minutes. Serves 4.

CAULIFLOWER WITH CHEESE SAUCE

1. Soak head of fresh **cauliflower** in salt water.

2. Drain and rinse. Place in large kettle and cover with **water,** add **salt** and boil gently until fork tender. Drain.

3. Place **2 Tbsp. butter** in pan. Add **1 heaping Tbsp. flour.** Melt and gradually add **milk** and **chunks of cheese**(about 1 inch of brick). Stir until melted and smooth. Pour over cauliflower and serve at once.

CHEESE SOUFFLÉ

1. Melt **4 Tbsp. butter** in deep pan, and add **4 Tbsp. flour.** (Make as a white sauce). Add **1 1/2 cups milk** and blend well. Add 1 1/2 cups **grated cheddar cheese** or Swiss cheese, stirring constantly until smooth.

2. Add **3/4 tsp. salt, a dash of white pepper, dash of Worcestershire sauce.** Stir well.

3. Remove from fire, and stir in **6 well beaten egg yolks.** Then pour into **6 stiffly beaten egg whites,** gently folding until blended.

4. Pour into greased 2 quart souffle dish.

5. With a teaspoon draw a line 1 inch from dish edge to form top hat.

6. Place in cold oven and set at 325° and bake for one hour. Serve immediately.

POTATO SOUFFLÉ

1. To **3 cups mashed potatoes,** whip in **1/2 cup cream** and **3 well-beaten egg yolks,** one at a time.

2. Season with **salt** and **nutmeg.**

3. Beat until stiff, **4 egg whites.** Fold into potatoes and turn into greased 1½ qt. souffle dish.

4. Sprinkle top with **grated Parmesan Cheese** and bake in 375° oven for 30 minutes or until well puffed and lightly browned.

5. Serve immediately. Serves 6 to 8.

MOTHER'S CHEESE DREAMS

1. Mix together **8 Tbsp. (1 stick) melted butter, 1 cup sour cream, 1/4 tsp. salt** and **1 1/2 cups sifted flour.** Refrigerate for 2 hours.

2. Mix in another bowl **1 1/4 lbs. (24 ozs.) large curd cottage cheese, 2 egg yolks, 2 Tbsp. melted butter** and **2 Tbsp. sugar.**

3. Chill. Divide dough into 4 parts.

4. Roll each part out as thin as possible on waxed paper or a floured board.

5. Put one fourth of the cheese mixture on one edge of each rolled out part of the dough. Beginning at the edge where the cheese is, roll up like a jelly roll. Tuck in the edges and put in a greased baking pan.

6. Rolls may be sliced before or after baking. Brush with melted butter and bake at 350° for 45 minutes or until golden brown.

BEER FONDUE

1. Heat **2 cups of beer** in a pan until almost boiling. Simmer until it cooks down.

2. In a bowl place **1 lb. grated cheddar cheese** and toss with **3 tablespoons of flour.** Toss well. Add to hot beer, stirring constantly and careful never to boil.

3. Add **1/4 tsp dry mustard, 1 tsp. Worcestershire sauce.** Stir constantly until all cheese has melted & is blended in.

4. Pour into fondue bowl and place over heat on fondue stand. Keep heat low under fondue and do not boil. Serve with **Italian** or **French bread** cut into bitesize cubes (with the crust on). Have each guest spear a piece of bread with a long-handled fondue fork and dip it into the fondue with a stirring motion until coated. Sprinkle **chopped chives** over top of fondue before serving. Serve with beer.

ZUCCINI AND TOMATOES

1. In large skillet, sauté **one large sliced onion, one large sliced zuccini squash** and **three cut up and peeled tomatoes** in **1/2 stick margarine.** Stir constantly, until done. Cook slowly.

2. Add **4 ozs. cheese** before serving, and place cover on skillet to melt. Serve hot.

CHEESE BLINTZES

Pancake batter:

1. Beat **4 eggs** well. Add **1 1/2 cups flour, 1/4 tsp. salt** and **2 Tbsp. melted butter.** Gradually add **2 cups milk.** Beat batter until smooth.

2. Grease skillet with butter. Using a 7 inch skillet, pour in three tbsp. of batter and tilt pan from side to side. See that batter covers bottom of skillet. Saute lightly on one side and then flip out of pan onto a paper towel or waxed paper.

Filling:

1. Mix together **1 lb. small curd cream cottage cheese, 1 egg yolk, 2 Tbsp. melted butter, 2 Tbsp. sugar, 1 tsp. vanilla** and **1/4 cup white raisins.**

2. Mix well the above ingredients. Place 1 Tbsp. filling in center of each blintz. Fold wrapper over on each side and then on each end.

3. You may place on waxed paper covered cookie sheets and cover with Saran Wrap and then foil and freeze until ready to serve.

4. When ready to serve, brown in skillet on both sides, in **butter or margarine.**

5. Serve with **sour cream** and **cherry preserves.**

Other Fillings:

1. Use canned or freshly cooked asparagus. Serve with hot cheese sauce poured over crepe. When adding filling, roll closed and do **not** fold ends.

2. Fill with Chicken a la King.

3. Use already prepared spinach souffle for filling.

4. Make cheese sauce. Add drained tuna and use as filling.

BAKED STUFFED POTATOES

1. Wash **potatoes** and cut a small slit in each one.

2. Bake for 1 hour at 450° or until done.

3. Remove from oven and cut in half lengthwise.

4. Scoop the potatoes from their jackets carefully.

5. Place potatoes in mixing bowl and add **milk** and **butter** and beat until smooth.

6. Fill jackets with whipped potatoes and sprinkle **grated cheddar cheese** on top.

7. Return to oven about 10 minutes before serving and bake until cheese melts. Serve at once.

KUGEL #1

1. Boil **1 10 oz. pkg. med. egg noodles** in salt water. Drain, pour cold water over them.

2. Mix together **16 oz. sour cream, 16 oz. cottage cheese, 6 eggs, beaten, 2 or 3 heaping tbsp. honey, 1/2 cup plumped white raisins** and a small amount of **dried apricots,** that have been soaked, drained, and cut up. **Thinly sliced apples** may be used instead of apricots.

3. Pour into a 9 × 13 well greased casserole. Mix **sugar** and **cinnamon** together and sprinkle generously on top.

4. Bake at 350° for 1 hour or until well done.

4. Bake at 350° for 30 to 45 min. or until well done.
KUGEL #2

1. Boil **1 10 oz. pkg. med. egg noodles** in salt water. Drain, pour cold water over them.

2. Mix together 1/3 cup of **margarine** and **1 heaping Tbsp. honey.** Add **6 eggs,** beaten, and stir into noodles. Add **1/2 cup raisins, 1 sliced apple** and **2 Tbsp. sugar.**

3. Mix all together and pour into well greased casserole. Mix **cinnamon** and **sugar** together and sprinkle thickly on top.

4. Bake at 350° for 30-45 min. or until done.

BROWN RICE AND MUSHROOMS

1. Place **1 cup natural brown long grain rice, 2 1/2 cups water, and 1 tsp. salt** in 3 qt. covered saucepan. Bring to a boil, stir, then lower heat to simmer.

2. In a large skillet brown **1 large diced onion** and **16 ozs. sliced fresh mushrooms** in **margarine.**

3. Cook rice about 40 minutes, simmering until all water is absorbed. Add rice to onion mixture and add more margarine if necessary. Brown all these together over low heat, stirring constantly. Serve hot.

ESCALLOPED POTATOES

1. Into greased shallow casserole, place a few **layers of potatoes,** thinly slice.

2. Sprinkle lightly with **salt.** Repeat over and over.

3. When dish is 3/4 full, pour **milk** over to almost cover.

4. Dot with **butter.**

5. Bake at 350° for 1 hour.

DAD'S POTATO PANCAKES

1. Grate or put through blender **4 large potatoes.**

2. Place grated potatoes in a bowl and add **1 large egg, 1/4 cup flour,** **salt** and **pepper** to season. Stir well.

3. Pour 1/4 inch of **peanut oil** in skillet and fry. After pouring batter for each pancake, smooth out with back of spoon until pancake is uni-from thickness. Brown on both sides. Serve immediately with sugar and cinnamon mixed and/or syrup.

HOLLANDAISE SAUCE

1. Heat **1 stick butter** until bubbly.

2. Place **4 egg yolks** and **3 tablespoons fresh lemon juice** in blender, turning it off and on quickly. Add a dash of **salt** and **white pepper.**

3. Turn blender on high and slowly add melted butter. Serve at once. This is delicious over asparagus or broccoli.

QUICK POTATOES

1. Heat **1 cup milk.**

2. Add **20-24 ozs. frozen, shredded potatoes** that have been thawed.

3. Cook until milk absorbs into potatoes.

4. Mix in **4 Tbsp. butter, 1 Tbsp. onion flakes, 1 tsp. salt** and a **dash of white pepper.** A little **finely chopped pimento** also, if you desire.

5. Pour in shallow buttered casserole or individual ramekins.

6. Sprinkle **grated cheddar cheese** on top.

7. Bake at 350° for 45 minutes to 1 hour or until brown. Serves 8.

POTATOES & ONIONS

1. In large skillet melt vegetable shortening to cover bottom of pan generously.

2. Add **1 or 2 onions thinly sliced** and cook for a few minutes.

3. Add **sliced potatoes, salt, pepper** and **paprika.** Place cover on skillet and cook until done and well browned, turning often.

POTATO SALAD

1. Peel and quarter potatoes. Place in kettle with water to cover. Shake in some salt. Cover & cook.

2. Boil until fork tender and drain well. Cool.

3. Place potatoes in large bowl. Add chopped **hard boiled eggs,** very finely **diced celery, chopped pimento** and **salad dressing.**

4. Mix together and add a little **sugar** and **salt** to taste and finely minced **green onions** (including greens).

5. Refrigerate in a glass bowl. Cover with waxed paper or Saran Wrap. Chill 2-3 hours.

6. Sprinkle with **paprika** and serve.

CANDIED SWEET POTATOES OR YAMS

1. Boil **6 large sweet potatoes** or **yams** until fork tender.

2. Remove from boiling water and peel. Quarter them and place in a loaf cake pan.

3. In large skillet melt **1 stick of margarine.** Add **1 large can crushed pineapple, light brown sugar** and about a **cup of orange juice** (or less). Cook gently until syrupy.

4. Pour syrup over the yams. Be sure each yam is coated.

5. Cover with **marshmallows.**

6. Bake for an hour or more, at 350° until marshmallows have disappeared and sauce has turned into candy.

SPANISH RICE

1. Place **1/2 stick butter** in top of the double boiler over water. Add **1/2 cup raw white rice, 1/2 tsp. salt,** and **1 cup water.**

2. Dice a **medium sized onion, 1 green pepper** and add to double boiler with **1 cup fresh tomatoes, peeled.**

3. Cook for 1 1/2 hours in top of double boiler, stirring occasionally. Serve hot.

CARROT RING

1. Cream together **3/4 cup shortening** and **3/4 cup brown sugar.**

2. Add **2 eggs** and beat together.

3. Mix together **2 cups sifted flour, 3/4 tsp. baking powder, 3/4 tsp. soda, 3/4 tsp. nutmeg,** and **1 tsp. cinnamon.** Add this to above mixture.

4. Add **2 cups raw grated carrots, 1 Tbsp. wine,** and mix well.

5. Bake in greased ring mold 1 hour at 350°. Serve hot. Center may be filled with peas and mushrooms together or with Brussels sprouts.

6. Use 6 cup ring mold.

CARROT TSIMAS

1. Peel and thinly slice **carrots** into rounds.

2. Place in pan with **salted water.** Boil until carrots are tender. Water should be cooked down into carrots.

3. Drain off most of water and add **several Tbsp. chicken fat** or **margarine. Add 2 Tablespoons honey** and **1/3 cup orange juice.**

4. Boil gently until carrots are glazed. Serve hot.

MUSHROOM SCRAMBLED EGGS

1. Wash **fresh mushrooms** and slice. Saute mushrooms in butter until golden brown. Remove from skillet and keep warm.

2. Beat **eggs,** add **milk** and **salt** and beat some more.

3. Melt **butter** in large skillet and pour in eggs. Cook gently over low heat, covered. Occasionally turn gently and when almost set, stir in mushrooms.

4. Serve hot. You may garnish with chopped parsley.

BROILED TOMATOES

1. Wash **tomatoes:** trim and stem ends, then cut crosswise.

2. Place each tomato half with cut side up on broiling pan.

3. Spread with **prepared mustard:** then sprinkle on **onion flakes** and **Worcestershire sauce.**

4. Sprinkle **buttered fresh bread crumbs** over tomato and a **dash of salt** on top.

5. Sprinkle **grated cheddar cheese** to top it all.

6. Broil until browned or cheese bubbles. Serve immediately.

CABBAGE & APPLES

1. Place **short ribs of beef** in deep kettle: then add **water** to cover.

2. Cut a small to medium size **head of cabbage** in chunks.

3. Peel and slice **4 apples.**

4. Add **1/3 cup brown sugar** and **salt,** and cook all together until done. Add a little **lemon juice** to taste and so it is sweet and sour.

5. Add a little **flour,** mixed in cold water, and cook until thickened. Serve hot.

BROCCOLI

1. Soak fresh **broccoli** in salt water. When ready to cook, drain and rinse again.

2. Boil gently in **salt water** until tender.

3. Pour **melted browned butter** over broccoli and serve with **fresh lemon.**

PRISMIK — EGGPLANT RELISH

1. Bake a **large eggplant** and **2 green peppers** until done.

2. Peel, remove and discard seeds from green peppers. Peel eggplant.

3. Chop together and add a clove or two of **garlic,** chopped fine.

4. Place in a jar and add a little **vinegar, salad oil,** and **salt** to taste. Mix well. Use **more oil than vinegar.**

5. Cover and refrigerate. Excellent with meat.

COLESLAW

1. Grate **1 medium size head of green cabbage, 3 carrots** and place in large bowl.

2. Drain a **20 oz. can of crushed pineapple** and add to cabbage.

3. Cut about a **dozen marshmallows** in fourths and stir in.

4. Add several heaping tablespoons of **mayonnaise,** until coleslaw is creamy. Refrigerate until ready to serve.

NATE'S KOSHER DILL PICKLES

1. Wash **cucumbers** well. Sterilize quart jars. (Dishwasher is great for this.)

2. Place small amount of **dill, 1/2 tsp. pickling allspice, small clove of garlic** on bottom of each quart jar.

3. Pack cucumbers in very, very tightly.

4. On top of cucumbers place the same ingredients and in the same quantities as you placed in bottom of jar.

5. Add **1 Tbsp. of salt** and **pinch of alum.**

6. Fill with cold water to about 3/4 inch from neck of jar.

7. Cover tightly and put upside down overnight to ensure no leaking.

8. Keep in a dark place for 3 months.

POTATO KUGEL

1. Peel and grate **6 potatoes** into salted water. Drain well.

2. Beat **2 egg yolks** and add **1 grated onion.** Add **4 Tbsp. matzo meal** (or 1/2 cup flour). Add **1 tsp. baking powder, 1 1/2 tsp. salt, 1/4 tsp. pepper** and **2 Tbsp. melted margarine** or **chicken fat.** Mix well.

3. Fold in **2 stiffly beaten egg whites.**

4. Pour into greased 1 1/2 quart baking dish or fill individual muffin tins 3/4 full. Pour **2 Tbsp. melted chicken fat** on top. Bake 375° for 1 hour or until mixture is set and lightly browned on top. Bake less if you are using muffin tins, about 40 minutes.

BAKED CELERY

1. Cut up **one stalk pascal celery** into 1 inch pieces. Place in large saucepan with **1/2 tsp. salt, 1/2 cup water** and heat to boiling point. Lower heat and cover and simmer for about 6 to 8 minutes.

2. Add **7 ozs. water chestnuts,** drained and sliced, **2 oz. jar drained,** and **diced pimentoes,** and **1/2 green pepper** diced.

3. Blend above with **one can cream of mushroom soup.**

4. Place in buttered casserole. Melt **1/2 cup butter,** add **1/2 cup slivered almonds,** and **1/2 cup bread crumbs** and sprinkle over above.

5. When it is room temperature, bake uncovered for 20 minutes at 350°.

SCRAMBLED EGGS AND LOX

1. Melt **4 tablespoons butter** or margarine in skillet. Add **3 chopped onions.** Saute' stirring frequently, (about 10 or 15 minutes).
2. Add **1/4 lb. smoked salmon,** cut in small pieces. Saute'.
3. Beat **8 eggs,** add **3 tablespoons water, salt** and **pepper** to taste, and pour over salmon mixture.
4. Cook gently over low heat, stirring constantly until set. Serve hot with toasted bagels and cream cheese.

CHEESE BLINTZE SOUFFLE

1. In flat casserole, place **1 stick margarine** and set in oven. Turn oven on to 350°. Watch until margarine melts.
2. Remove casserole from oven and tilt so that all of dish is covered with melted margarine.
3. Beat **5 egg yolks.** Add **1 1/2 cups sour cream** (12 oz.), pinch of **salt, 1/2 cup orange juice, 1 tsp. vanilla** and beat until smooth. Set aside.
4. Place **16 blintzes** in casserole. Then turn each one over so that both sides are buttered.
5. Lightly sprinkle with **light brown sugar.**
5. Beat **5 egg whites** until stiff. Fold into egg batter. Pour over blintzes. Lightly srinkle again with **light brown sugar** (or a mixture of **sugar** and **cinnamon,** if desired).
7. Bake about 40 minutes or until golden brown. Serve warm as is or with fresh fruit berries or cherry preserves. Serves 12.

SOUR CREAM CUCUMBERS

1. Sprinkle **2 teaspoons salt** on **3 cucumbers** that have been peeled and sliced very thin. Set aside for 30 minutes, turning occasionally. Drain thoroughly.
2. Mix together **1 cup sour cream, 3 tablespoons cider vinegar, 1/8 teaspoon white pepper, 1 teaspoon sugar,** and **2 teaspoons chopped dill.**
3. Chill for 1 hour and serve as a relish.

MANICOTTI WITH CHEESE

1. Purchase **manicotti shells** already made. In a large bowl place **2 lb.** ricotta cheese, 2 eggs, 1/3 cup parmesan cheese, 8 ozs. grated mozzarella cheese, 1/8 tsp. white pepper, 1 tsp. salt, 1 tablespoon chopped parsley and mix well.

2. Pour 1/4 cup into each manicotti.

3. In a large skillet saute' **1 large diced onion, 2 cloves of garlic** that have been put through a garlic press, in **margarine.**

4. Add a **2 lb. can of Italian tomatoes,** a **6 oz. can of tomato sauce, 1 1/2 cups water, 1 tablespoon salt, 1 tablespoon sugar,** shake in a little **oregano,** and **1/4 tsp. pepper.** Mash with a fork. Bring to a boil and simmer, covered, stirring occasionally for about 40 minutes.

5. Grease 2, 13x9 casseroles. Pour 1 1/2 cups tomato sauce into each pan. Place manicotti, seam side down in pan. Pour remaining sauce over top and sprinkle each pan with **1/2 cup grated parmesan cheese.** Bake covered with aluminum foil for 1 hour in 350 degree oven. Serve hot.

SWISS FONDUE

1. Peel a **garlic clove** and rub inside of fondue pot with it. Discard garlic.

2. Place **1 lb. Swiss** and **Gruyere cheese grated** (half of each) in a bowl and toss with **3 tablespoons of flour** to coat cheese.

3. Heat **2 cups dry white wine,** but do not boil. Gradually add cheese and stir until all cheese is added and melted and sauce is smooth, being careful to keep at a simmer and never to boil. Stir in **3 table-spoons kirsch, 1 tablespoon of fresh lemon juice,** shake in a little **white pepper.** You may add a **dash of nutmeg** and **cayenne pepper** if you desire. If you prefer you may add **fruit brandy** instead of kirsch.

4. Pour into fondue pan, if you have not already cooked this in it, and place over heat on fondue stand. Keep heat low under fondue still careful not to boil. Serve with **Italian or French bread** cut into bitesize cubes (with the crust on). Have each guest spear a piece of bread with a long-handled fondue fork and dip it into the fondue with a stirring motion until coated. Serve the same wine to drink that you have made the fondue with.

CREAMED SPINACH

1. Wash and pick over **10 oz. of fresh spinach** in cold water. Place spinach in saucepan. (Do not add water.) Lightly sprinkle with **salt.** Cover pan and bring spinach to a boil, turn heat to low and simmer until wilted and tender. Drain.

2. Add **1 tablespoon butter, 3 ounces cream cheese,** place cover on pan and return to stove. Warm until cheese melts. Stir, squeeze on **fresh lemon juice,** and serve at once. Makes four small servings.

MACARONI AND CHEESE

1. In 2 quarts boiling water, pour in **7 ounces macaroni.** Bring to a boil and cook for about 8 minutes or until tender.

2. Drain and pour cold water over for a few minutes.

3. Butter a 1½ quart flat casserole. Layer macaroni alternatively with **Velveeta Cheese** chunks and **butter** in between. Pour **milk** over to the top level. Bake 350° until milk bakes in and it is light brown, about 60 minutes.

PASTA SALAD

1. Boil **16 ounces of Rotini** in salt water, add a spoon of oil.

2. Cook fresh **broccoli flowerettes** for a short period until tender but retains bright green color. Drain.

3. Sauté **2 or 3 garlic cloves** (that have been pressed through a garlic press) in **olive oil.** Add **8 ounces (or more) sliced fresh mushrooms** and diced **red sweet pepper.**

4. Mix drained and blanched Rotini with sautéed ingredients in a large bowl. Add sliced small **red sweet onion, fresh snipped dill** and lots of **grated parmesan cheese** or aged white cheddar. You may add **sliced black olives,** or use your own imagination. Serve warm (at once) or cold.

VEGETABLE MARINADE

1. In a large measuring cup or bowl with spout, place these ingredients:
   ¾ cup virgin olive oil
   4 tablespoons tarragon vinegar
   1 teaspoon fresh snipped dill weed
   ½ teaspoon paprika
   2 or 3 fresh cloves of garlic (pressed)
   ½ cup peanut oil
   ½ teaspoon dry mustard
   fresh basil
   dash white pepper

2. Mix all together and pour into à jar.

3. Drain canned tiny Belgian carrots. Cook whole frozen green beans until tender, but still retains bright green color. Drain white asparagus and artichoke hearts, also hearts of palm.

4. Place all vegetables in relish platter and pour marinade over. Vegetables may be marinated over night in a flat bowl. To serve, sprinkle with snipped dill weed.

Fish

FISH

Index

GEFILTE FISH

1. Take 2 1/2 to 3 lbs. **lake trout,** 1 1/2 lbs. **pike,** 2 lbs. **white fish** and clean and filet. You should have about 4 lbs. of fileted fish. Grind fish with **2 large onions.**

2. Place **heads, bones** and **skin** into a large kettle with **3 medium size onions, 1 carrot, 2 teaspoons salt,** and **1/2 teaspoon white pepper,** with **water** to cover and boil, then simmer to make a broth. After a rich broth is made, remove bones, skin and heads and discard them leaving the hot broth in kettle.

3. While this is cooking, make fish balls. In electric mixer place ground fish and onions. Add **5 eggs, 3 teaspoons salt, 3/4 teaspoon white pepper, 2 tablespoons Matzo meal,** and **1 cup water.** Start with just 1 cup of water, adding it slowly while you are beating. If fish seems too soft, use less water. You may use up to about another 1/4 cup of water if necessary. Beat well, working it all together as well as you work dough to make bread. It should get firm and fluffy.

4. Wet your hands and make into balls and place in hot fish broth. Add **celery tops** and **2 carrots.** Simmer for 3 to 4 hours. When done gently remove to a large flat platter, and pour broth over the fish balls and chill. Serve with horseradish or mustard.

TUNA FISH SALAD

1. Drain **2 cans of Albacore tuna fish** and place contents in a bowl.

2. Very finely dice **celery** and add to tuna fish.

3. Add **2 or 3 hard cooked eggs,** cut up.

4. Add **mayonnaise** and mix together.

5. Place a lettuce cup on salad plate. On lettuce cup place a large ring of pineapple or a half an avacado or a tomato and fill with tuna fish salad. Garnish with ripe olives. Serves 4 to 6.

BAKED FRESH SALMON or WHITEFISH

1. Place cleaned **whole salmon** in shallow baking pan lined with aluminum foil (enough to cover).

2. **Salt, pepper,** and **paprika** inside and out. Slice **1 small onion** and place in fish. Spread a little **butter** inside. Sprinkle **flour** lightly over outside of salmon, and place one stick of butter over top of fish. Pour dry white wine over salmon and lemon juice over whitefish.

3. Bake about 400° around 30 to 40 minutes or until it starts to brown. Then lower heat to 325 or 350° and pull aluminum foil over to cover. Bake several hours until fork tender.

4. Serve with lemon wedges and fresh parsley and melted seasoned butter from pan poured over it, or Lemon Butter Fish Sauce.

5. If desired, gently remove skin and glaze.

STUFFING FOR FISH

1. In large bowl place **4 cups bread cubes.**

2. In skillet brown **chopped onion** and **diced celery** in **stick** of **margarine or butter.**

3. Pour browned onion, celery and all of butter in skillet into bread cubes. Season with salt and pepper. Add **3 eggs,** beat a little water into them and mix well.

BAKED SALMON (CANNED)

1. Empty **1 tall can** of **red Alaska Sockeye salmon** into bowl. Remove bones and flake with fork.

2. Beat **3 eggs** and add to salmon. Then break up **12 white crackers,** or **2 slices egg bread broken up,** dice **a small onion,** and add. Pour **1/2 cup milk** into mixture and stir.

3. Pour into greased casserole, place **lumps of butter** on top and bake for 45 minutes to one hour at 350°.

4. Salmon is finished baking when a knife inserted in center comes out clean.

SWISS CRAB BROIL

One Dungeness Crab serves 6 people.

1. Remove crabmeat from crab.

2. Take 6 slices of bread and trim all 4 sides. Butter the top of the slice of bread and toast lightly. Sprinkle crabmeat over toasted bread; then spread a thin coating of mayonnaise over this. (You may add a little prepared mustard to mayonnaise if desired).

3. Then top with a slice of tomato and a slice of Swiss cheese and broil. (You may use New York Sharp cheese in place of Swiss cheese).

CRAB LOUIS

1. Line salad plates with bibb lettuce leaves.

2. Shred iceberg lettuce and arrange on leaves.

3. Place crabmeat, in chunks, atop the lettuce.

4. Circle with tomato wedges and hard boiled egg slices. Top with claw meat from crab.

5. Pour Louis Dressing on top of each salad. Sprinkle with paprika and garnish with ripe olives.

LOUIS DRESSING

1. Combine 1 cup mayonnaise, 1/4 cup chili sauce, 1/4 cup chopped green pepper, 1/4 cup sliced green onion with tops, and 1 tsp. lemon juice and dash of salt.

2. Fold in 1/4 cup whipped cream.

LEMON BUTTER FISH SAUCE

1. In a medium size bowl grate the rind of 1 lemon, add the juice of 1/2 lemon, 1 stick soft butter, dash of salt and dash of white pepper.

2. Whip together with a fork. Then using a whisp, gradually whip in a little whipping cream. Pour over fish or pour in sauce bowl, snipping parsley on top.

CRAB QUICHE

1. Sprinkle **1 cup shredded Swiss cheese** (4 ounces) evenly over bottom of **pastry shell**.

2. Drain and flake **one 7 1/2 oz. can crab meat** and sprinkle over cheese.

3. Slice **2 green onions** (top and all) thinly over crab meat.

4. In a small bowl combine **3 beaten eggs, 1 cup light cream, dash of salt, 1/2 tsp. grated lemon peel, 1/4 tsp. dry mustard** and a **dash of mace.** Mix well adding **sherry** to taste, and pour over ingredients in pie shell.

5. Bake at 325° for 45 minutes or until set.

6. Remove from oven and let stand 10 minutes before serving.

CRAB STUFFED AVOCADO OR PAPAYA

1. Mix **1/4 cup mayonnaise, 1 Tbsp. chopped chives,** dash of **salt** and **pepper,** dash of **Worcestershire sauce** and **1 1/2 Tbsp. lemon juice.**

2. Mix **1 cup crabmeat** (or a 7 oz. can) lightly into dressing. Chill.

3. Halve **2 avocados** lengthwise and remove pits. Pare avocado halves. Place in or brush with **lemon juice** or grapefruit juice to retain color. If using artichoke. Cook and then fill.

4. When ready to serve, fill avocado halves with crab salad. Sprinkle with **riced hard cooked eggs.** Place on lettuce cup and garnish with **slices of orange** and **grapefruit** and **ripe olives.** Serve dressing of your choice over it.

SHIRLEY'S SALMON RAMEKINS

1. In 1 1/2 quart saucepan, over medium heat melt **6 tablespoons butter.** Stir in **6 tablespoons flour** until blended. Gradually stir in **2/3 cup half and half,** and **1/4 cup white wine,** and cook stirring constantly.

2. Remove bones from a **1 lb. can of sockeye salmon** and break up a bit with a fork. Add salmon, with it's liquid, **1 cup grated Swiss cheese** and a **4 ounce can of drained mushrooms,** sliced.

3. Spoon salmon mixture into six greased 10 oz. ramekins. Top each with heaping tablespoons of **Swiss cheese.**

4. Bake at 350 degrees for 15 minutes, or until hot and bubbly.

LOBSTER THERMIDOR

1. Boil **1 large box frozen rock-lobster tails** in salted water until done. (as directed on pkg.)

2. Clip membranes and remove from shells. Snip lobster tails into chunks.

3. Melt **6 Tbsp. butter** in top of double boiler. Stir in **1 tsp. salt, 1/4 cup flour, 1/8 tsp. nutmeg, dash of paprika** and **3 Tbsp. sherry.**

4. After this has started to cook, put in lobster and cook until mixture thickens.

5. Pour in shells — you may use the lobster shells or something similar.

6. Sprinkle with **grated cheddar cheese** and broil for a short time or until cheese bubbles.

7. Serve immediately with cocktail forks.

LOBSTER SALAD

1. In **lettuce cup** put **diced celery** that has been mixed with a little **mayonnaise.**

2. Sprinkle **diced hard boiled egg** over this.

3. With kitchen shears, cut **lobster** that has been boiled, drained, emerged in cold water and removed from the tails and chilled, into large chunks.

4. Mix lobster with a little **mayonnaise** and squeeze **fresh lemon juice** over this.

5. Place generous portion on top of the eggs. Twist a **lemon slice** over this and serve.

CREAMED TUNA FISH

1. In large skillet melt **1/2 stick butter;** add **1 Tbsp. flour,** then slowly add **milk.** Stir to keep smooth.

2. Add **Cheez Whiz** or **Velveeta Cheese** and stir until it melts.

3. Add **1 can drained albacore tuna.** Break up with fork slightly and cook a few minutes.

4. Serve on toast, over Chinese Noodles, or in patty shells. Place buttered toast points in individual souffle dishes and pour tuna over it.

TUNA MOUSSE

1. Soften **1 1/2 envelopes** (1 1/2 Tbsp.) **gelatin** in **1/2 cup cold water.** Add **1/4 cup lemon juice.**

2. Heat and stir over medium heat until gelatin is dissolved.

3. Stir into **1 cup mayonnaise.**

4. Add **2 cans** (7 oz. size) **albacore tuna, 1/2 cup chopped cucumber, 1/2 cup finely diced celery,** a little **finely chopped pimento, 2 tsp. onion juice, 1 tsp. prepared horseradish,** pinch of **salt, 1/4 tsp. paprika.** Mix well. Fold in **1 cup cream, whipped.**

5. Pour into individual molds for a luncheon or for a buffet pour into a fish mold. Chill until firm. Unmold and garnish.

MOLDED FISH

1. 1. Simmer **1 cup tomato juice, 1 tsp. whole mixed spices, 1 tbsp. sugar,** and **1/4 tsp. salt** together for 5 minutes. Strain.

2. Soften **1 tbsp. gelatin** in **1/2 cup cold water** for 5 minutes, then dissolve in hot tomato mixture. Add **3 tbsp. lemon juice** and cool.

3. When gelatin mixture begins to thicken, fold in **1/3 cup of celery** and 1 1/2 cup cooked fish, flaked. (I use a large size can of Red Alaska Sockeye Salmon.)

4. Pour into fish mold and chill until firm. Use olives for fish eyes.

5. Remove from mold and serve on lettuce covered platter.

RED SNAPPER WITH BANANAS

1. Melt **1/2 stick unsalted margarine** in a 9 × 13 pyrex pan.

2. Lightly **salt** and **pepper** cleaned and fileted halves of a **red snapper.** Place skin side down in melted margarine in pan.

3. Slice a **banana** on each half. Place a thin slice of **margarine** over each of the banana slices.

4. Bake at 400° for 15 minutes, then reduce oven to 350° for 45 minutes more or until done.

CAVIAR

Make an **omlet** — spread with **sour cream** and **red caviar**. Fold in half and serve.

Top salads with **black caviar**.

Whip **cream cheese** with milk until very light. Put **cottage cheese** through ricer, then whip in blender with cream cheese until light. Place on serving dish, cover top with **black caviar, squeeze lemon juice** over **caviar**. **Rice egg yolks** and **whites** separately and garnish with them. Serve with **bread rounds** or **crackers.**

SHRIMP THERMIDOR

1. In saucepan melt **1/4 cup butter.** Stir in **1/4 cup flour, 1 cup light cream, dash of salt, dash of white pepper** and **1/4 cup sherry.**

2. Cook while stirring, over low heat, until sauce thickens.

3. Remove from heat and add **1 1/2 lbs. shrimp** (shrimp should be cleaned, cooked and split). You may substitute 1 lb. flaked white crabmeat or 1 lb. lobster flaked instead of shrimp.

4. For a buffet party, pour into buttered 10" x 6" x 2" baking dish or 6 individual ramekins.

5. Sprinkle with **1 cup shredded cheddar cheese.**

6. Bake at 425° for 10 minutes or until cheese melts.

You may make in large seashells and use for hot hors d'oeuvres.

STUFFED TOMATOES WITH SHRIMP

1. Peel **tomatoes** and scoop out center.

2. In skillet, brown in **butter** finely diced **onion;** then add **cooked rice,** the center of the tomato you have scooped out and **shrimp.** Brown these together and fill tomatoes with mixture.

3. Top with **bread crumbs** and/or **grated cheese** and bake.

SHRIMP SAUCE

Combine the following ingredients to taste: **chili sauce, lemon juice,** and **horseradish.**

TROUT or SALMON FILET en CROÛTE

1. Place cleaned **whole fileted fresh fish** in a shallow baking pan lined with aluminum foil paper, and cup it around fish. **Salt, pepper** and **paprika** inside and out. Slice **1 onion** and place in fish. Cut **slices of butter** and place inside fish. Sprinkle **flour** lightly over outside of salmon and place a sliced **stick of butter or margarine** on outside of fish.

2. Bake at 400 degrees for 60 minutes or longer. Remove fish from oven. Cool.

3. Thaw out a package of frozen **puff pastry** and roll it to a thickness of 1/8 inch. Place the fish in the middle of the pastry and completely encase it. If possible, remove skin from fish and pour butter over the top. Place back in pan in another sheet of aluminum foil. Roast at 400° for 15 minutes and then turn oven to 350 degrees for 45 minutes longer. Serve hot, with fresh **lemon wedges.** Whip **1 egg yolk** with a **little water** and paint the top of the crust before baking.

SALMON MOUSSE

1. Drain a **1 lb. can sockeye salmon** and reserve juice.

2. In small saucepan place one **8 ounce package cream cheese,** and the contents of **1 can of tomato soup.** Heat and stir together until melted.

3. Dissolve **2 packages gelatin in 1/2 cup cold water.** Add to soup and cheese and mix well. Pour into a bowl and add **1/2 cup salmon juice, 1 small finely grated onion, snipped dill weed** and **finely diced red pepper.**

4. **Add 3/4 cup buttermilk, 1/2 cup mayonnaise** and mix well. Stir in salmon and **finely snipped parsely.** Pour into greased fish mold and refrigerate. Serve cold with sauce of **whipped cream,** dash of **salt,** dash of **sugar,** and a little **horseradish.** For variety, substitute **1 cup Hidden Valley Dressing** made with **buttermilk** for mayonnaise and buttermilk above.

5. Makes a large fish mold or 6 large individual molds or 8 small molds.

SHRIMP CLEMENCEAU

1. Peel 5 or 6 medium size **potatoes.** Cut into eighths and boil in water, enough to cover with salt added.

2. Meanwhile, place 1 stick **butter or margarine** in large skillet and when melted add a **clove or two of garlic** that has been put through a garlic press. Add one large diced onion and saute', stirring constantly. Add medium or small size **shrimp.** As many as desired.

3. When potatoes are fork tender, drain and cut again with fork into smaller pieces, and add to skillet. Stir until shrimp and each potato is coated with garlic butter. Strain a small **3 oz. can of tiny peas** and a **3 oz. jar of sliced mushrooms** and stir in.

4. Serve hot with fresh snipped parsley on top.

POACHED SALMON IN ASPIC

1. In a fish poacher make a wine court bouillon by combining **1 quart of dry white wine, 1 quart water, 1 tablespoon salt, 2 small carrots, 1 thinly sliced large onion,** and **a bouquet garni.** The bouquet garni should be tied together or placed in an enclosed stainless steel ball, consisting of **12 peppercorns, 2 cloves, 3 bay leaves,** some **sprigs of parsely,** and some **celery tops.** Bring to a simmer. Then simmer for 30 minutes.

2. Place cleaned **salmon** on rack or in cheesecloth and lower into bouillon. Poach a 6 lb. salmon for about 1 hour. Ten minutes to the pound. Never let it boil—just simmer.

3. When done let it cool in its cooking liquor. When you lift fish out of pan, strain broth and then add **1 package gelatin** and return to stove and bring to a boil. Stir.

4. Spoon thin layer of aspic over fish, let aspic set, then decorate. Chill. Then pour more aspic jelly over fish and let set in refrigerator.

5. Pour remaining jelly in bowl and refrigerate. Whip before serving. Lay salmon on this bed of whipped aspic on a fish board or platter, and garnish with **stuffed eggs,** thin sliced **lemon** and **watercress.** Decorate fish with **pimentoes, truffles,** and **olives.** Serve with Cucumber Dill Fish Sauce.

GRAVAD LAX

1. In a 9 × 13 glass pan, place a layer of **fresh dillweed.**

2. Mix together **1/2 cup Kosher salt, 1 tablespoon white pepper,** and **1/3 (heaping) cup of sugar.**

3. Clean and fillet a fresh 4 lb. **salmon** and then slice in half lengthwise.

4. Rub some of the salt mixture into skin side of salmon, then place skin side down on a bed of dill. Rub salt mixture on up side of salmon fillet. Place fresh dill over this. Rub salt mixture on both sides of remaining fillet. Place on top of other fillet and cover skin with more dill.

5. Cover with heavy plastic wrap. Take the next size glass pan and place on top of salmon. Fill with canned goods to weight it down.

6. Marinate in refrigerator 24 to 30 hours, basting at 12 hour intervals, inside and out. Then turn over entire fish as though it is in one piece each time you baste it.

7. Remove from marinade and wipe dry with paper towel.

8. Serve cold with skin side down on board and gently slice thin. Slice with a wide French knife and at an angle. Do not cut through skin. Serve with pumpernickle bread and mustard sauce, or tiny boiled potatoes.

9. Make a mustard sauce by mixing together prepared mustard, lemon juice, fresh snipped dill and a little oil. Add mayonnaise if you wish a creamy type of sauce.

CUCUMBER DILL FISH SAUCE

1. Peel and slice thin **1 large cucumber** and remove seeds. Place in shallow pan and sprinkle with **salt.** Place another plate over cucumbers, for weight. Refrigerate and keep draining, for 24 to 36 hours.

2. Cut into small pieces. Mix with 16 ounces **sour cream.** Snip in fresh dill weed. Squeeze fresh **lemon juice** and mix in. Finely slice green onions, greens and all. Stir well and serve cold with fish.

Meats

MEATS

Index

MEATS

BEEF FILLET en CROÛTE

1. Place a **beef tenderloin** in a shallow pan that has been lined with aluminum foil paper. Cup foil around meat. Pour a little **oil** and **sweet red wine** over meat. Sprinkle with **garlic salt** and **lemon pepper**.

2. Roast at 450 degrees for 20 minutes. Remove meat from oven and cool until room temperature.

3. In a large skillet place **1 large diced onion** and a **cup of sliced mushrooms** and brown together in **oil**.

4. Thaw out a package of **frozen puff pastry shells** and roll to the thickness of 1/8 inch. You may use my **pie crust recipe** instead if you desire. Place filet in the middle of pastry and spread browned onions and mushrooms over meat. Pull pastry over meat to completely encase it, wet edges and seal tightly. Place the pastry wrapped beef in a baking pan and paint the top with an **egg yolk** whipped with a little **water**.

5. Bake in 500 degree oven for 20 minutes or until golden brown. If you do not wish to place the mushroom and onion mixture on the meat, you may serve it as a sauce with the meat later or even thicken a little with a little cornstarch and water.

BRISKET A LA GORDON

1. Place **brisket of beef**, fat side up in a shallow pan. Pour about a third of a bottle of **liquid smoke** over meat. Add a little water to the pan. Sprinkle garlic salt and grind fresh pepper over top of meat.

2. Roast at 300 or 325° for about two hours.

3. Pour a **large can** of **tomato sauce** over the top of the meat, then sprinkle generously with **brown sugar**. Squeeze the juice of half a **lemon** over this and sprinkle a little **Worcestershire sauce** on it.

4. Roast 350° still uncovered for several hours until very tender. Omit liquid smoke if desired. You can not overcook. Roast for hours until very tender. Be sure there is always liquid in pan.

SWISS STEAK

1. Trim excess fat off **2 lbs. round steak** cut 1 1/2 to 2 inches thick.

2. Combine **flour, salt** and **pepper** and pound this mixture into both sides of meat.

3. Heat a little **oil in a large skillet, then brown meat quickly on both sides.**

4. Combine **2 cups canned tomatoes, 1 or 2** (as desired) **cups diced onions,** and a sprinkle of **garlic salt.** Pour this over meat.

5. Cover, turn burner to hot and when it starts steaming, turn down to low and cook for 1 1/2 hours or until meat is tender.

6. Remove meat and thicken gravy with **2 Tbsp.** of **flour** mixed with **1/4 cup cold water.** Add a **Tbsp. of sugar.** Cook a few minutes and pour over meat and serve. Serves 6-8 people.

CHARCOAL BROILED TENDERLOIN

1. When coals are hot, place whole tenderloin on grill.

2. Grind fresh pepper over it, sprinkle on garlic salt.

3. Keep turning until seared. Wrap in aluminum foil and broil longer — until it is cooked as rare or well done as desired.

FLOMEN TSIMAS

1. In a large shallow pan place a **brisket of beef,** fat side up. Sprinkle **garlic salt** and **lemon pepper** on it.

2. Place about **8-10 very small whole peeled carrots, celery tops,** and **2 oz. (340 grams) large pitted prunes** around roast. Add **water** to cover bottom of pan.

3. Roast uncovered 325 degrees. After an hour, place about **6-8 small potatoes** around brisket. Sprinkle **salt** and **paprika** on each one.

4. Turn oven up to 350 degrees and roast several hours longer, occasionally turning potatoes, and be sure there is always liquid in pan. Must be well done. Roast until very tender when tested with a fork.

SPAGHETTI WITH MEAT

1. Boil **1 lb. of spaghetti** in **salt water** to which **1 tablespoon of oil** has been added.

2. In skillet brown in oil, **1 diced onion, 2 ribs of diced celery, 1 diced green pepper** and **1 lb. fresh mushrooms,** and 3 pressed **garlic cloves.**

3. Then add **2 lbs. of ground beef,** season with **garlic salt** and fresh ground pepper, and sprinkle in **oregano.**

4. When this is all browned together, pour over spaghetti in baking dish.

5. Add **2 28 oz. cans of stewed tomatoes** and **1 8 oz. can of tomato sauce.** Mix well. Sprinkle with **cheese** on top.

6. Bake in 350° oven until it all cooks together.

LEG OF LAMB

1. Place **leg of lamb** in shallow pan. Cut slits in top of lamb and put slices of **fresh garlic** in them. Season with **salt, fresh ground pepper, and paprika.**

2. Lightly sprinkle a little **flour** on lamb. Pour a small amount of **water** in pan. Place two or three **carrots** and some **celery tops** in the pan.

3. Roast at 325°. Place in oven early and roast until very tender for many hours.

4. After it is in the oven several hours, place **potatoes** around the lamb. Salt and paprika each potato.

5. An hour or less before serving, place **peach halves** in pan and a heaping spoon of **mint jelly** in each one. Roast close to an hour longer.

PLUM SAUCE FOR LEG OF LAMB

1. Drain **1 lb. can** or (2 cups) **purple plums,** reserving 1/4 cup of the syrup. Pit and sieve plums.

2. Combine the **1/4 cup of syrup, plums, 2 Tbsp. lemon juice, 1 Tbsp. soy sauce, 1 tsp. Worcestershire sauce,** and **1 clove crushed garlic.**

3. Baste lamb with plum sauce that has been seasoned with garlic, salt and pepper in 325° oven. Roast until well done.

BARBECUED LAMB BREAST

1. Place **lamb breast** (ribs) in 500° oven and bake for 20 minutes to remove fat. Drain.

2. Over ribs pour this sauce: **1 grated onion, 1/2 cup chili sauce,** juice of half a lemon, **3 Tbsp. Worcestershire sauce, 3 tsp. paprika, 1 cup tomato juice, 4 tsp. brown sugar, 1/2 tsp. salt, 2 tsp. dry mustard** and juice of **1 can pineapple chunks.**

3. Bake 300° for 3-4 hours, basting often until meat falls from bone. If sauce dries up, add either tomato juice or pineapple juice.

4. About 15 minutes before it is done, add pineapple chunks to cook in sauce.

ESIK FLEISHE

1. Cut into cubes **1 fat round steak** or rib steak 1 or 2 inches thick.

2. Add **salt, pepper** and an **onion.**

3. **Cut up carrot** in small pieces, add a little **water, 1/2 cup ketchup** and a little **sugar.**

4. **Cook like stew, but do not use potatoes.**

BARBARA'S CHICKEN APRICOT

1. Combine in a bowl **1 bottle Russian dressing, 1 package onion soup mix** and **1 jar apricot preserves.**

2. Place **1 whole cut up fryer** in a shallow pan skin side down. Pour half the sauce over the chicken. Bake at 325° for 25 minutes. Then take chicken out of oven and turn it over.

3. Pour remaining half of the sauce over chicken. Bake for an additional 50 to 60 minutes. Serve hot.

CHUCK'S RANCHO BEANS

1. In a large skillet cook **2 cups diced onions** in a little **oil** or **margarine** until done (turn yellow).

2. Add **1 lb. ground beef, 1/2 tsp. salt** and cook and stir until beef is well done.

3. Add **1 cup catsup, 2 Tbsp. red wine vinegar, 2 Tbsp. mustard, 2 Tbsp. brown sugar, 1 large can vegetarian beans,** and **1 can kidney beans,** well drained. Cook until ingredients are well mixed and serve hot.

STUFFED CABBAGE ROLLS

1. Carefully remove **leaves** from **cabbage.**

2. Pour **boiling water** over separated leaves.

3. Take small cabbage leaves that are too small to be filled and place in bottom of deep kettle.

4. Mix together **2 lb. ground round steak** or chuck with **1/4 cup rice,** that has been partially cooked, **3 eggs, slightly beaten, garlic salt** and **pepper** seasoned to taste. Mix well.

5. Make meat balls; wrap each meatball in a cabbage leaf and place in kettle. After kettle is half full, slice a **large onion** on top of this. Pour in a large can of **tomatoes.** Finish placing the rest of the meat in the cabbage leaves. Makes about 14 cabbage rolls.

6. When you have finished filling the kettle with all of the cabbage rolls, pour a large can of tomato sauce over the top. Squeeze **juice of half a lemon,** and sprinkle **one half or three-fourths** of a **cup of brown sugar** over this.

7. Cook on top of stove slowly for hours until very well done over a low heat.

8. When done, either serve hot or refrigerate in a pyrex bowl and heat in oven slowly for several hours. They are better the next day!

JANET'S GANTSE TSIMAS

1. Toss **2 1/2 lbs. stew meat** (2 inch cube size) in **seasoned flour.** Brown in **oil** in deep stew pot over high fire. When meat is almost browned, add **1 large chopped onion** to brown.

2. Add **parsley, celery greens, salt, pepper, bay leaf, thyme,** and **1 can of beer.** Bring to a simmer. Cook over very low flame for 2 1/2 hours. Remove parsley and celery.

3. Squeeze **1 lemon** and blend the juice with **1/3 cup brown sugar.** Mix with hot stew juice. Return to pot along with **24 prunes, 12 whole, cooked baby carrots** (canned Belgium are excellent), **3 potatoes,** quartered lengthwise, and cook for 1/2 hour more.

4. Near serving time, place in oven proof low casserole, the meat decorated with the prunes, and baby carrots surrounded by the potato quarters. Pour stew sauce over everything. Cover with foil and heat and serve. Garnish with **parsley.** It's marvelous!

APPLE STUFFED VEAL ROLLS

1. In large skillet melt **1/2 stick margarine**. Add **1 finely chopped onion;** sauté, stirring often, until golden.

2. Add **two cups soft bread cubes, 1 thinly sliced** (and peeled) **apple.** Cut each slice in half and add dash of **salt, pepper** and **1 egg beaten.** Cook and stir for about 4 minutes.

3. Place **1 heaping tablespoon** stuffing on each thin veal slice; roll up. Secure with toothpick.

4. Roll in flour seasoned with salt and pepper.

5. Heat a couple more **tablespoons margarine** in skillet and brown rolls on all sides.

6. Add **3/4 to 1 cup apple cider** (or apple juice) simmer, covered, about 35 minutes, or until tender.

7. Remove picks, spoon juices over veal. Makes 8 veal rolls.

STUFFED BREAST OF VEAL

1. **Breast of veal with pocket** - season with **garlic salt** and **pepper.** Place in roaster with **1 onion** and **2 carrots.**

2. Pour water over **half a loaf of stale bread** and mash water off through strainer.

3. Grate **2 large potatoes** and **brown diced onion** in chicken fat or oil, salt and pepper to taste. Add bread, drained and **2 eggs.** Mix well.

4. Stuff in pocket and roast for a very long time until well done at 350°.

PRIME RIB OF BEEF

1. In shallow pan place **standing rib roast,** standing with fat side up. Cut slits and place **garlic cloves** in them or just sprinkle with **garlic salt.** Grind **fresh pepper** and sprinkle **paprika** over roast.

2. Add a **cup of water** to pan, **2 or 3 whole peeled carrots, celery tops** and a **quartered onion** if desired. Roast, uncovered, at 325°.

3. Later, add **peeled whole potatoes** that have been sprinkled with salt and paprika.

4. Do not overcook. This roast should not be served well done. Roast 20-25 minutes per pound.

ROAST CHICKEN

1. Place **cut up chicken** in pan with **sliced onion, whole carrots, celery tops** (a little fat if necessary).

2. **Salt** and **paprika** each piece.

3. After it roasts for 30 minutes, add less than a cup of water.

4. Roast at 350° and keep turning.

5. When half done, place **peeled Irish potatoes** in pan with chicken. Salt and paprika each potato.

GARLIC BROILED CHICKEN PAPRIKASH

1. Split broilers, wash and shake water off.

2. Place chickens on barbecue grill. Sprinkle with **paprika** and **garlic salt.**

3. After 5 minutes turn chicken and season other side.

4. Continue turning until well done.

SHERRY BARBECUED CHICKEN

1. Dip **2 cut up frying chickens** in **flour** seasoned with **salt, paprika** and a pinch of **pepper.**

2. Saute chicken in **margarine** until golden brown on all sides. As each piece is done, remove and place in long shallow pan.

3. When all chicken is removed from pan, add **1 bottle ketchup, 1/3 cup margarine, 1/2 cup sherry, 1/2 cup water, juice of one lemon, 1 Tbsp. onion flakes, 1 Tbsp. Worcestershire sauce, 2 Tbsp. brown sugar** and the remainder of the seasoned flour. Bring this to a boil.

4. Pour this sauce over chicken and cover pan with aluminum foil. Bake at 325° for 1 1/2 hours or until very tender. Serves 6.

CHICKEN PIE

1. Place **1 cup flour, 1/2 teaspoon salt, 2 teaspoons baking power,** and **1/4 cup shortening (Crisco)** in food processor. Blend for a few seconds.
2. Add **1/3 cup water** through tube. Blend until a ball forms. Divide into two parts.
3. Place on floured board and pat (do not roll) into circle and fit into an 8 inch deep pie pan.
4. Make Chicken Ala King (page 110). Pour into pie shell.
5. Pat top shell out and place on top. Pinch around edges and pierce top shell with fork.
6. Bake 450° for 20-25 minutes or until golden brown. Serve hot. May be frozen before baking. Serves 4 to 6 people.

ROAST TURKEY
Bread Dressing:

1. In large bowl place **bread crumbs,** use 2 lb loaf of dried egg bread.

2. In large skillet, brown **1 large diced onion** and **2 cups diced celery in salad oil.** Pour into bread crumbs.

3. Beat **4 or 5 eggs** and a little water, with a fork.

4. Pour eggs into bread crumbs. Mix dressing and season with salt and pepper. Do Not make very moist!

---

1. Wash turkey, inside and out. Stuff cavities with dressing and sew with dental floss. Tie legs together. Salt turkey well.

2. In a bowl place **2 heaping Tbsp. flour.** Pour **salad oil** over and mix until thin mixture. Spread all over turkey, then sprinkle with **paprika.** Add about **2 cups water** to pan.

3. Roast for 30 minutes at 450 to 500 degrees. Then turn down to 350 or 325 and roast around 4-5 hours or until nice and brown and very tender. Baste.

4. Remove turkey from roaster and place on serving platter. I place my platter on my hot tray and cover turkey with heavy aluminum foil until ready to serve.

5. Place roaster on burners of stove. In small bowl place **2 heaping Tbsp. flour.** Add cold **water** to thin and pour this in pan. Add a couple of glasses of **hot water.** Stir and scrape the brown drippings on the side of pan until dissolved. This makes brown gravy. Stir and boil well. Strain and serve.

ROAST QUAIL IN SHERRY

1. Clean **quail** throughly and soak in salt water overnight.

2. Rinse birds well. **Salt** lightly and place a lump of **margarine** in each bird.

3. Mix **flour** and margarine together and rub over birds.

4. Place in baking pan and bake 325° for 1 hour. Put a little **water, sherry wine** and **melted butter** in pan; add 1/4 tsp. **marjoram** and baste frequently. Can be stuffed with bread or rice dressing if desired.

5. Serve on buttered toast. If you do not make dressing, Brown Rice and Mushrooms is delicious with quail.

TURKEY ASPIC

1. Sprinkle **2 envelopes unflavored gelatin** on **1 cup** of **chicken broth** in saucepan.

2. Place over low heat and stir until gelatin is dissolved.

3. Remove from heat and stir in remaining broth (Use 2 cans 10 1/2 oz. each condensed chicken broth. Take out 1 cup for Step #1).

4. Stir in **1 cup white wine.**

5. Pour half of the mixture into a 13 x 9 x 2" pan. Chill in refrigerator until almost firm.

6. Arrange a **slice of hard cooked egg** and an **oval slice of turkey breast**-and do this all over the gelatin mixture. Spoon gelatin over each egg slice before you top with turkey.

7. Spoon remaining gelatin over top. Be sure to keep slices in place. Chill until firm or overnight.

8. Cut into rounds, leaving an aspic edge on each slice. Place on toast rounds. For a cutter for toast and aspic, take a #2 1/2 can and remove ends. Bend into oval shape.

9. Lift out with pancake turner. Line plate with lettuce first, put down oval toast (or bread). You may put dressing on this if desired. Then place oval of aspic turkey on it.

10. Garnish with ripe olives, radish roses and tomato wedges.

11. Place them just on lettuce bed if you do not wish any bread, or make them tiny and cut with biscuit cutter. Toast and aspic and use for canapes.

ROAST TURKEY BREAST

1. Wash and salt **turkey breast.** Place skin side up in shallow pan. Place **tops** of **celery, with leaves,** under turkey breast.

2. In a small bowl place **2 tablespoons flour.** Pour **salad oil** over flour and mix until a thin consistency. Spread over turkey and sprinkle with **paprika.** Add water to pan to cover bottom of pan.

3. Roast 30 minutes at 450 degrees. Turn oven to 350 degrees for 2 1/2 more hours or until tender and brown.

ROAST DUCK

1. Place cleaned **duck** in shallow baking pan. Pour **orange juice** over duck. Sprinkle with **salt** and **paprika.** Roast 2-3 hours at 425° for duck 3 1/2 to 5 lbs.

2. After duck is roasting, prick skin all over with fork so that the fat will run out. Do this several times.

3. Pour **mandarin oranges** over duck, including the juice, and roast until well done. If desired, stuff with bread dressing that has an apple sliced in, or serve with BROWN RICE AND MUSHROOMS.

ORANGE GLAZE FOR DUCK OR CHICKEN

1. Combine **2 Tbsp. thinly slivered orange peel, 1/4 cup orange juice, 1/2 cup light corn syrup** and **1/4 tsp. ginger. Pitted bing cherries** may be added.

2. Brush ducks or chickens with glaze and roast 15 minutes. This glaze is put on after the fowl is done — just roast 15 minutes longer with it on.

3. Let stand in this glaze a few minutes before carving.

KAFTELAS

1. Boil **2 large chicken breasts** until tender. Remove white meat and put through grinder. Grind **1 onion,** separately, using coarse disc or grater. Sauté onion in chicken fat or margarine.

2. Add **2 eggs,** a little **salt** and make into patties about the size of a silver dollar.

3. Sauté lightly — just enough to brown.

4. Empty contents of **one quart jar of beet borscht** into kettle. Slice in a small **onion** and add juice of **1/2 lemon.** If desired, add sugar. Heat, add patties and cook gently.

5. Serve hot in boullion cups.

CHICKEN A LA KING

1. In large skillet place a **heaping Tbsp. flour, Tbsp. chicken fat** (or margarine).

2. Turn stove on lowest burner and stir these together. Gradually add chicken soup.

3. Add cut up, **cooked chicken breast**, **diced pimentos, sliced mushrooms** and **canned drained peas.**

4. Cook all together. Add more soup or a little water if necessary.

5. Serve hot in patty shells or on toast.

TONGUE

1. Rinse **cow** or **calves tongue** and place in kettle covered with **cold water.** Add **1 onion, 2 carrots, pickling spices, salt** and **pepper.**

2. Cover and boil gently until fork tender.

3. Peel and slice. Serve hot or cold.

FILLET OF BEEF BORDEAUX

1. Place **beef tenderloin (whole)** in a shallow pan that has been lined with aluminum foil paper. Cup the foil on all sides of the meat.

2. Pour **1/4 cup dry red wine,** and **1/4 cup oil over meat.** Sprinkle a little **soy sauce** over it. Shake **garlic salt** and **lemon pepper** over top and sides of filet.

3. Roast at 425° for 40 minutes. Baste at 15 minute intervals. The center will be pink.

4. 1 and 3/4 lbs. tenderloin serves 4 people. 3 and 1/2 to 4 lbs. serves eight people. Cook the same for both.

5. Slice meat and serve with its own juice. Saute **fresh mushrooms** and spoon over meat.

BRANDY PEPPER STEAK

1. Pan broil a very tender **top sirloin steak.** When done grind or shake **coarsely ground pepper** on both sides to coat steak.

2. While pan is still hot, turn off fire and pour in **1/4 cup brandy or cognac.** Ignite with a long handled match. Be sure to use a long handled match or you may burn your arm off!

3. Turn steak while brandy flames. When flame goes out, place steak on board and slice thickly. Put on platter and pour all of the brandy over steak. Scrape **pepper** from bottom of pan onto steak.

This is fast and exquisite. Turn out the lights when you flame it and watch the expression on your guests face.

CALVES LIVER AND ONIONS

1. Slice **2 large onions.** Place in skillet with melted **vegetable shortening.** Cook gently, turn occasionally.

2. Wash and shake dry **4 to 6 slices of calves liver.** Dip both sides in flour that has been seasoned with **salt** and **pepper.**

3. Move onions aside with fork and add floured liver. Cover and fry gently first on one side and then the other until done.

HAMBURGERS

1. Place **1 lb. ground chuck or round steak** on board. Take **1 slice of stale bread** and soak with cold water. Mash this into meat. Whip up **1 egg** with fork and mash this in. Season with **garlic salt and pepper.** Wet hands and make into patties. Makes 4 or 5 large ones.

2. Gently fry in a covered skillet. Serve hot in bun. Do **Not** use any grease to fry.

RACK OF LAMB

1. Sprinkle **rack of lamb** with **garlic salt, lemon pepper,** and place in shallow pan, fat side up.

2. Place in 450° oven for about 25 minutes, or until seared and fat is brown. Reduce heat to 350° and finish roasting until done. Usually 30 minutes per pound.

3. Place on platter and garnish rib ends with **paper frills.** Plan usually on two ribs per person. Serve hot with **mint jelly.**

111

BRISKET HASH

1. Boil **4 to 6 potatoes** until almost tender. Use amount of potatoes in proportion to meat amount. Drain potatoes.

2. In skillet brown a very **large onion** that has been diced, in **chicken fat** or margarine.

3. Cut boiled potatoes into small pieces, the size of a quarter. Add potatoes to onions in skillet and more chicken fat, if necessary, and brown.

4. Put **cooked left over brisket**, through meat grinder. When meat is all ground up, mix in skillet with potatoes and onions. Be sure and pour in all of the **juice from meat** and also **babecue sauce** from brisket.

5. Bake 30 minutes or longer at 350°. Serve hot.

MANICOTTI WITH MEAT

1. Saute **1 large diced onion**, and **2 cloves of garlic** that have been put through a garlic press, in **margarine**.

2. Add a **2 lb. can of Italian tomatoes, a 6 oz. can of tomato sauce, 1 1/2 cups water, 1 Tbsp. salt, 1 Tbsp. sugar**, and shake in a little **oregano**, and 1/4 tsp. pepper. Mash with a fork. Bring to a boil and simmer, covered, stirring occasionaly for about 40 minutes.

3. In a large skillet saute **1 large diced onion**, add **1 1/2 lbs. ground chuck**. Season with **garlic salt** and **pepper** and cook until nicely brown. Place in **manicotti shells**.

4. Grease two 13 x 9 casseroles. Pour 1 1/2 cups of tomato sauce into each pan. Place filled manicotti, seam side down, in pan. Pour remaining sauce over top. If you desire sprinkle 1/2 cup grated **parmesan cheese** over top. Bake covered with aluminum foil for 1 hour in 350° oven. Serve hot.

CURRIED GINGER CHICKEN SALAD

1. Cook **breasts of two chickens** until tender. When cold remove from bone and cut in chunks. Place in bowl and add finely cut up **rib of celery**.

2. In **half a cup of mayonnaise**, mix ¼ **teaspoon mild curry powder**. You may use more mayonnaise and ⅛ teaspoon of curry if you wish. Cut up **crystallized ginger** (as much as desired) and mix all ingredients together.

3. Serve on lettuce and garnish with grapes that have had lemon juice squeezed over them and dipped in granulated sugar. For regular chicken salad, omit curry and ginger, add cut **pimento**, mix salad and serve in half a **papaya**, or **avocado**.

CHICKEN SAUTÉ FACILE

1. Place **1 stick margarine** in 13 x 9 loaf pan. Place in 325° oven until it melts. Remove at once.

2. Turn oven to 425°. Wash and clean cut up **young chicken.**

3. On a sheet of wax paper, place about a **cup of flour.** Shake on **salt** and **pepper** to season.

4. Dip each piece of chicken, on both sides, in this flour mixture; arrange skin side down in melted margarine, and sprinkle with **paprika.**

5. Set pan in oven for 20 minutes. Remove from oven and turn each piece and again sprinkle with paprika. Return to oven for 20 minutes again. Turn once more and leave in turned off oven for another 5 or 10 minutes. Serve immediately.

CHICKEN KIEV

1. Wash and pat dry, **6 boned, skinned chicken breasts** that have been split in half.

2. Into **2 sticks of softened margarine,** press **2 or 3 cloves of garlic** through your garlic press. Add **freshly chopped parsley** and finely **snipped chives** and a little **salt.** Mix well and place in aluminum foil and freeze so that it can be cut into 12 pieces.

3. Place chilled margarine mixture in chicken breast and fold lengthwise. Fold in the ends and fasten with a toothpick.

4. Whip **3 eggs** well. Dip chicken in eggs and then into **bread crumbs** or **matzo meal.**

5. Fry in **oil** until brown on both sides. Place on paper towels to drain, using tongs, and then place in pan in oven and bake at 200° for 15 minutes, or until done.

6. To freeze just wrap in freezer foil and later when you wish to serve, heat frozen in 350° oven for 30 minutes.

—

Pies

PIES

Index

MY PIE CRUST

1. Mix **3 cups flour** together with **1 tsp. salt**, add **1 cup vegetable shortening**. (Rinse cup with cold water before measuring shortening)

2. Blend together with pastry blender.

3. Make a well in center of batter and pour in **1/2 cup cold water**.

4. Mix with spoon very well.

5. Sprinkle a little flour on baking board.

6. Divide dough into 4 equal parts. Roll out.

7. Makes 2 double crust pies or 4 pie shells.

8. For one double crust pie, just cut ingredients in half.

9. Bake a single shell, after making air holes with fork, 425° for 5-8 minutes until light brown.

LEMON-ORANGE PIE

1. Combine **1 cup sugar, 3 Tbsp. corn starch, 1/4 cup orange juice,** and **1/4 cup lemon juice** in saucepan.

2. Beat **3 egg yolks** and add to mixture.

3. Stir in **1 1/4 cups boiling water** gradually. Heat to boiling directly (do not use double boiler). After it has started to boil, cook very gently for 4 minutes stirring constantly.

4. Pour this into a 9 inch baked pie shell.

5. Beat **4 egg whites** until stiff, but not dry.

6. Gradually beat in **8 Tbsp. sugar** and **a heaping 1/4 tsp. cream of tartar** and a pinch of **salt**. Spread meringue over pie.

7. Brown in 400° oven until golden brown. Serve cold.

APPLE PIE

1. Peel, core and slice **8 apples** or more to make a full pie.

2. Place apples in pastry lined pie pan.

3. Sprinkle with **3/4 cup sugar** and **nutmeg**. You may add just a **dash** of **cinnamon**.

4. Place top crust on pie (make a design first with knife and fork for air holes).

5. Place a small amount of cold water completely around edge (between layers).

6. Fold edge under. Press around edge with fork or finger.

7. Bake at 450° for 15 minutes, then turn down to 350 for 45 minutes or until golden brown.

CHERRY PIE

1. Mix in saucepan, **1 cup sugar, 1/4 cup flour, 1/2 tsp. cinnamon, 1/2 cup fruit juice** (from canned cherries).

2. Cook over medium heat stirring constantly, until mixture thickens and boils.

3. Pour hot thickened juice over **3 and 1/2 cups drained, pitted, sour, water packed cherries** (**2 cans**). Mix lightly.

4. Pour into **pastry-lined pie pan** and cover with lattice top crust.

5. Bake at 425° for 35 to 45 minutes.

FRESH PEACH PIE

1. Peel and slice **8 large fresh peaches**. Add a few drops of **almond flavoring** and **1 1/4 cups sugar**. Place in pie shell and cover with top crust.

2. Bake at 450° for 15 minutes. Then reduce heat to 350° and bake 45 minutes to an hour.

PINK GOOSEBERRY PIE

1. Head and tail **1 heaping quart gooseberries.**

2. Place gooseberries, **2 cups sugar,** a little **water, juice of 1/2 lemon or less,** and a **little orange juice** in a saucepan and cook until berries are softened.

3. Pour into bowl and let cool several hours in refrigerator until thick.

4. Bake in double crust at 450° for 15 minutes, then reduce heat to 350° and bake 45 minutes.

5. Cool and serve.

BLUEBERRY PIE

1. Prepare **1 quart or more fresh blueberries.** Add **1 1/4 cups sugar** for a 10 or 11 inch pie.

2. Bake in double crust 30 minutes at 425° then 350° for 30 more minutes or until done.

3. Serve with soft vanilla ice cream.

4. Freeze blueberries in season by washing, draining well, and storing in plastic containers. Do not fill to top. Leave 1/4" of room in container from top.

CREME DE MENTHE PIE

1. Make chocolate crust for pie shell of **chocolate wafer crumbs or 24** crushed chocolate wafers. Mix with **4 Tbsp. melted butter** and press into 8" pie shell.

2. Melt **7 oz. jar marshmallow creme** with 1/2 cup milk in double boiler.

3. Cool. Stir in **4 Tbsp. Green Creme de Menthe** and **2 Tbsp. White Creme de Cacao.**

4. Fold in **1 cup whipped cream.**

5. Shave **semi-sweet chocolate** over top.

6. Freeze. Then serve frozen.

FRESH STRAWBERRY PIE

1. Combine 1 1/2 cups crushed strawberries, 3/4 cup sugar and 2 to 3 Tbsp. lemon juice. Let stand 30 min.

2. Soften 1 Tbsp. unflavored gelatin in 1/4 cup cold water and dissolve over hot water.

3. Add to the fruit mixture and chill until partially set.

4. Fold in 1 cup heavy cream, whipped.

5. Pour into graham cracker crust.

Graham Cracker Crust

1. Crush 12 cracker. Add 1/3 cup sugar and 1/2 cup melted butter. Mix well.

2. Press firmly into pie pan. Chill until set. Fill.

RHUBARB CUSTARD PIE

1. Peel and clean rhubarb. Pour boiling water over 4 cups of rhubarb that have been cut into 1/2 inch pieces. Drain after 5 minutes.

2. Beat 3 eggs and add 3 Tbsp. milk.

3. Mix and stir in 1 1/2 cups sugar, 1/4 cup flour and 3/4 tsp nutmeg.

4. Mix rhubarb in. Pour into pastry lined pan. Cover with lattice top. Bake 375° for 50 min.

GRAHAM CRACKER PIE

1. Roll 17 graham crackers until fine (or use packaged crumbs). Mix in 1/2 cup melted butter and 1/2 cup sugar. Set aside one cup of mixture. Press into pie pan, like a crust. Set aside.

2. Meanwhile, add 2 cups scalded milk to 4 Tbsp. cream corn starch and 1/3 cup sugar. Cook over water until thick; then add 2 egg yolks and cook 2 minutes more. Add 1/4 tsp. almond extract and pour into pie shell.

3. Beat two egg whites with 4 Tbsp. sugar until stiff and cover pie with this.

4. Sprinkle cup of reserved crumbs and smooth off with knife.

5. Bake 325° for 20 minutes. Cool and serve.

KEY LIME PIE

1. Thoroughly mix **1 Tbsp.** (1 envelope) **unflavored gelatin, 1/2 cup sugar** and **1/4 tsp. salt** in saucepan.

2. Beat together **4 egg yolks, 1/2 cup lime juice,** and **1/4 cup water;** stir into gelatin mixture. Cook over medium heat, constantly stirring until mixture comes to a boil.

3. Remove from heat and stir in **1 tsp. grated lime peel.** Add a drop or two of green food coloring to give a pale green color.

4. Chill, stirring occasionally, until mixture mounds slightly when dropped from a spoon.

5. Beat **4 egg whites** until soft peaks from, then add **1/2 cup sugar.** Fold gelatin mixture into egg whites. Fold in **1 cup whipped cream** and pour into baked pastry shell.

6. Spread with additional **whipped cream** and edge with **grated lime peel.** Center with **grated pistachio nuts** and garnish with **lime wedges.**

BANANA CREAM PIE

1. Melt **2 Tbsp. butter.** Blend **1/4 cup cream corn starch, 3/4 cup sugar** and **1/2 tsp. salt.** Add **2 cups milk** gradually. Heat to boiling over direct heat.

2. Stir into **2 slightly beaten egg yolks.**

3. Return to heat and cook 2 min. Stir constantly. Add **1 tsp. vanilla.**

4. Slice **3 bananas** in baked pie shell and pour cooled cream filling over them. Chill.

5. Before serving, **whip cream** with **powdered sugar** and spread over the top.

RHUBARB MERINGUE PIE

1. Blend well together **2 Tbsp. butter, 1 1/2 cups sugar, 1/2 cup flour,** and **1/4 tsp. salt.**

2. Blend in **3 beaten egg yolks** until well mixed.

3. Peel and clean rhubarb. Pour boiling water over **4 cups diced rhubarb.** Drain after five minutes.

4. Combine rhubarb with above mixture. Pour in an unbaked 9-inch pie shell. Bake at 350° for 40 minutes.

5. Beat **3 egg whites** with **6 Tbsp. sugar** and spread this meringue on warm pie. Bake at 400° for 8 to 10 minutes or until brown. Cool before serving.

HEAVENLY PIE

1. Line pie plate with pastry and bake 375° for 12 minutes.

2. Mash **2 ripe bananas** through a potato ricer (or blender). Place in mixing bowl and add **1 cup sugar, 1/8 tsp. salt** and **2 (unbeaten) egg whites.**

3. Beat all together until stiff and frothy. Add a few drops **almond extract** and mix well.

4. Pour into baked pie shell. Bake for 30 minutes at 375°.

5. Remove and chill thoroughly.

6. Top with **1/2 pint of whipped cream** with **1/4 tsp. vanilla** mixed in.

7. Dot the surface with cubes of **currant jelly** and sprinkle with **1/4 cup chopped nuts.**

CHOCOLATE MOCHA ANGEL PIE

1. Beat **3 egg whites** (that have been standing at room temperature) until stiff.

2. Add **1/4 tsp. cream of tartar, dash of salt** and **3/4 cup granulated sugar** and beat until stiff and satiny.

3. Spread 2/3 of meringue over bottom and sides of well greased 8" pie plate. Drop remaining meringue, in mounds, along rim of pie plate. Make a point on each mound.

4. Bake at 275° for one hour. Shell should be light brown and crisp. Cool on rack.

5. Combine **1/4 cup boiling water** and **1 Tbsp. instant coffee.** Then stir in **2 cups melted** (over hot water) **chocolate chips.** Stir well, then cool for 5 minutes, stirring occasionally.

6. Fold this chocolate mixture into **1 cup heavy cream whipped** that has **1 tsp. vanilla** added.

7. Pour into meringue shell and refrigerate.

CHOCOLATE CREAM PIE

1. Pour **2 1/2 cups milk** in top of double boiler.

2. Drop in **3 tubes or squares melted, unsweetened chocolate** and blend together.

3. Mix **1 cup sugar, 5 Tbsp. flour** and **1/2 tsp. salt** and stir into chocolate mixture. Stir constantly until thickened. Cook ten minutes.

4. Mix a small amount into **3 slightly beaten egg yolks** and stir into remaining hot mixture. Cook 2 minutes longer. Continue stirring.

5. Add **2 Tbsp. butter** and **1 tsp. vanilla.**

6. Cover and cool.

7. Pour into pie shell. Cool before cutting and top with whipped cream.

CHOCOLATE CANDY PIE

Shell

1. Press 12 inch square of foil into 9" pie pan to form shape of pan. Lift foil onto ungreased cookie sheet carefully. Heat oven to 350°.

2. Pour in 6 oz. pkg. semi-sweet chocolate pieces and 2 Tbsp. butter. Bake 2-3 minutes. Return foil to pan and smooth mixture over bottom.

3. Refrigerate 5 minutes or until cool enough to spread on sides of pan. Smooth up to inside edge of pan with back of spoon. Coat entire pie pan carefully and evenly.

4. Refrigerate 25 minutes. Lift foil from pan and set on table. Peel foil from sides. Hold in palm of hand and peel away rest of foil quickly.

5. Replace shell in pie pan. Keep cold.

Peppermint Chiffon Filling

1. Soften 1 pkg. gelatin in 1/2 cup cold water. Cook over boiling water until dissolved. Cool.

2. Beat 3 egg whites stiff. Beat in 1/4 cup sugar gradually until firm peaks form. Mix in gelatin gently.

3. Fold in 1 cup whipped cream to mixture and add 1/2 tsp. peppermint extract and 1/2 cup crushed peppermint candy. Spoon into finished pie shell and refrigerate until firm.

WALNUT PIE

1. In large mixing bowl, place 6 eggs, 1 cup liquid brown sugar (or 2 cups light brown sugar), 1 1/2 cups corn syrup. Beat well.

2. Melt 3/4 stick butter and beat in with 1 teaspoon vanilla.

3. Sprinkle 3/4 cup walnuts (broken) in bottom of 10 or 11 inch unbaked pie shell. Pour mixture on top. Cover top of pie with walnut halves.

4. Bake at 375° for 1 hour. Pie is done when filling is firm when gently shaken.

HOT CARAMEL MOCHA PIE

1. Butter a 9 inch pie pan. Beat **3 egg whites** with a **pinch of salt**, and 1/2 tsp. **cream of tartar**, until stiff. Beat in **1 cup sugar**.

2. Add **20 Ritz or High Ho crackers** that are slightly crumbled, and fold in. Add **3/4 cup broken English walnuts** and fold in.

3. Pour into pie pan and bake 25 minutes at 350°. Cool.

4. Soften **1 quart of coffee ice cream** slightly and place in cold crust. Freeze.

5. When ready to serve cut each piece and place on dessert plate. Top with hot caramel sauce with broken pieces of English walnuts.

Hot Caramel Sauce

In saucepan combine **1 cup packed dark brown sugar, 1/2 cup light corn syrup**, and **2 Tbsp. of butter**. Heat slowly to a boil, stirring constantly. Place cover on saucepan for a minute until all sugar crystals melt on sides of pan. Uncover. When all sugar is dissolved, remove from heat and cool slightly. Slowly add **1/2 cup cream** and **1/2 tsp. vanilla** and mix well. Add **English walnuts** for above dessert and stir more. Makes close to 2 cups.

FUDGE PECAN PIE

1. In double boiler top, over water, melt **2 squares unsweetened chocolate**. Remove from heat and water, and add **1/2 cup packed, brown sugar**, and **1/4 cup butter**. Beat until well blended together.

2. Add **1/2 cup granulated sugar**, and mix well. Add **3 slightly beaten eggs**, **1/4 tsp. salt**, and **1/4 cup corn syrup**. Beat very well. Slowly stir in **1/2 cup milk**. Cook over water again, stirring constantly for about 5 more minutes.

3. Remove again from water and stir in **1 cup broken pecans** and **1/2 tsp. vanilla**.

4. Pour into 9 inch **unbaked pastry shell** and bake 350° for about 50 min. Remove from oven and sprinkle **1/4 cup broken pecans** on top and return to oven and bake 5 or 10 minutes longer until done. Serve warm with **ice cream** or **whipped cream**.

PECAN PIE

1. In large mixing bowl place **1 cup light brown sugar**, packed, and **3 eggs** and beat well.

2. **Beat in 3/4 cup corn syrup, 1/4 tsp. salt, 1/2 stick melted butter,** and **1 tsp. vanilla.** Beat very well together.

3. Place **1/2 cup broken pieces of pecans** on bottom of **unbaked pastry shell.** Pour above mixture into pie shell. Garnish top of pie with **1/2 cup of pecan halves.** For an 8 or 9" pie shell.

4. Bake 375° for 30 to 40 minutes. It is done when filling is firm in center when gently shaken. Cool. Serve with **whipped cream.**

PUMPKIN PIE

1. In large mixing bowl place **2 eggs,** and **3/4 cup sugar** and beat well. Add **two cups of fresh cooked** and **mashed** (I put it in a blender and whip up after cooked) or use **canned pumpkin, 1 lb.** can. Then add **1/2 tsp. salt, 1/2 tsp. ginger, 1/4 tsp. cloves, 1/4 tsp. nutmeg,** and **1 tsp. cinnamon.** Add **1 2/3 cups light cream** or **evaporated milk** and gently mix altogether until well blended.

2. Pour into 9 inch **unbaked pastry shell** and bake at 425° for 15 minutes and then reduce heat to 350° for 45 minutes. Pie is done when knife inserted in center of pie comes out clean.

3. Top with **whipped cream** that has a little **confectioner's sugar** whipped into it.

Cookies

COOKIES

Index

BUTTER COOKIES

1. Soften **1/2 cup butter** (1 stick) to room temperature. Into butter tho roughly mix: **1/2 cup sugar, 1 cup flour, 1 egg yolk, pinch of salt, 1 tsp. brandy** (or vanilla).

2. Pinch off small pieces of mixture and roll into balls, the size of large marbles.

3. Place on cookie sheet. Make a small depression in each. Fill this with **currant jelly** (or preserves).

4. Bake at 350°. Watch carefully so they do not burn, about 20 or 30 minutes. Makes 2 dozen.

HOLIDAY BUTTER COOKIES

1. Cream **1 pound soft butter**, add **1 cup sugar**, and beat well. Then add **2 egg yolks**, slightly beaten.

2. Add **2 Tbsp. brandy**, then **6 cups flour** with **1 tsp. baking powder** mixed in, and mix well. Use only enough flour to handle.

3. Chill dough several hours, then roll and cut with small biscuit cutter.

4. Brush with **2 beaten egg whites** and press a piece of **candied cherry** in each cookie. Then sprinkle with sugar.

5. Bake at 350° for 10 to 15 minutes.

DELICATE LEMON BARS

1. Place **2 cups flour** and **1/2 cup confectioners' sugar** into bowl. Cut in **1 stick butter** and **1 stick margarine**. Blend with pastry blender.

2. Lightly grease 14 x 10″ loaf cake pan. Press mixture into pan and bake 20 minutes in a 350° oven.

3. While this is baking, beat **4 eggs, 1 1/2 cups granulated sugar,** and **1/3 cup fresh lemon juice** together well. At lowest speed, blend in **1/4 cup sifted flour** and **1/2 tsp. baking powder.** Pour over baked shortbread and bake 25 minutes longer in 325° oven.

4. Sift **confectioners' sugar** over it when done. When cool, cut into bars.

HOLIDAY TORTE

1. In large mixing bowl, place 2 cups light **brown sugar,** 1½ cups **shortening, 4 eggs** and beat well.

2. Add ½ cup **orange juice,** ¼ tsp. **salt.** Beat well.

3. Add **4½ cups flour** and **3 tsp. baking powder** and slowly beat until smooth.

4. Grease loaf pan 9 × 13, and pour in ½ of batter.

5. Spread with tart jam (I use plum jam). Pour remaining batter over this. Bake 350° for 60 minutes.

6. Immediately on removing from oven, sprinkle with a mixture of **cinnamon** and **sugar** over top of torte. Wait 5 minutes and cut diagonally so that the pieces will be diamond shaped.

STRAWBERRY ALMOND KRUMKAKE

1. Beat **3 eggs,** add **1/2 cup of sugar** and beat well.

2. Add **1/2 cup** very **soft butter, 1/2 cup flour** and **1 tsp. almond flavoring.** Mix well.

3. Heat krumkake iron. Every time before using krumkake iron, wash and dry well first. Grease iron once before the first cookie, but not before each cookie. Heat iron to moderate heat.

4. Place teaspoonful of dough on iron and bake until very light brown.

5. Roll quickly on cone or press into patty shell. If using cone, pinch closed on one end.

6. Before serving, fill with **fresh strawberries** and **whipped cream.**

QUICK SUGARPLUMS

1. Dip marshmallows in warm milk.

2. Roll in colored sugar.

MOM'S HOLIDAY TWISTED COOKIES

1. Melt and cool 1/2 lb. butter.

2. Add 1/2 pint cream, 3 egg yolks, break up 2 pkgs. yeast and add to mixture. Add 2 1/2 cups flour and mix. Place bowl in refrigerator overnight.

3. Beat 3 egg whites stiffly. Keep in refrigerator.

4. Roll half of dough on baking board and place rest back in refrigerator. Roll to pie thickness.

5. Spread half of egg whites over rolled out dough. Mix crushed walnuts with sugar and cinnamon and sprinkle over egg whites. Repeat with other half of dough & egg white.

6. Cut in strips and twist into figure 8's or any shape desired.

7. Place on cookie sheet. Bake at 375° from 5 to 10 minutes or until golden in color.

ORANGE TEA WAFERS

Dough:

1. Mix 1 cup (or 2 sticks) soft butter, 1/3 cup thick sour cream, and 2 cups sifted flour together. Chill.

2. Roll out 1/8 inch thick on floured cloth-covered board. Cut with 1 and 1/2 inch round cookie cutter. Roll only a third of dough at a time, keeping rest refrigerated.

3. Transfer cookies to piece of waxed paper, heavily covered with granulated sugar.

4. Place cookies on ungreased baking sheet; prick with fork about four times. Bake 8 to 10 minutes in 375° oven. Sprinkle with colored sugar crstals.

Filling:

1. Blend 1/4 cup (1/2 a stick) soft butter with 3/4 cup powdered sugar, sifted, one egg yolk, 1 tsp. vanilla, and 5 drops of orange extract.

2. Put two cookies together with filling. Makes 5 dozen cookies.

SOUR CREAM DROP COOKIES

1. Cream 1 cup butter, 2 cups sugar.

2. Add 3 eggs, 1 cup sour cream, 2 Tbsp. brandy (or vanilla). Beat well.

3. Add 4 cups sifted flour, 2 tsp. baking powder, 1/2 tsp. soda, 1 tsp. salt and 1 tsp. nutmeg. Blend together.

4. Add 1 1/2 cups broken walnuts or pecans.

5. Drop from teaspoon onto greased cookie sheets, 2 inches apart.

6. Combine 1/4 cup sugar and 1 tsp. cinnamon in a shallow dish.

7. Butter bottom of a glass; dip into sugar cinnamon mixture and flatten each cookie.

8. Bake at 350° for 15 minutes. Makes about 6 or 7 dozen large cookies.

DATE BARS

1. Blend 3/4 cup vegetable shortening, 1/2 tsp. cinnamon, 1/4 tsp. cloves, 3/4 tsp. salt, 1/4 tsp. nutmeg. Add 1 1/2 cups brown sugar, drop in 2 eggs. Mix well.

2. Add 1 cup raisins, 1/2 cup chopped nuts, 1 cup cut up dates.

3. Mix 3/4 tsp. soda in 2 1/4 cups flour. Add this alternately with 1/4 cup fruit juice. Mix well.

4. Bake at 370° in greased loaf pan for 25-30 minutes.

5. Cut into bars.

APRICOT OATMEAL SQUARES

1. Mix together 1 1/2 cups raw quick cooking oats, 1 cup light brown sugar, 1/2 teaspoon baking soda, 2 cups flour and 1 cup ground pecans.

2. Melt 3/4 cup butter and pour over above mixture.

3. Pour 2/3 of this into a 10 × 14 greased pan.

4. Mix 1 large jar of apricot preserves with 1 tablespoon water and 2 tablespoons fresh lemon juice. Pour this over oatmeal crust. Top with remaining oatmeal mixture.

5. Bake at 350° for 30 to 40 minutes. Cut while warm and freeze. Sprinkle with powdered sugar before serving.

HAMENTASHEN

1. Cream together 1/2 lb. **very soft butter** and two **8 oz. packages of cream cheese** that are at room temperature. Beat until light and fluffy.

2. Stir in **2 cups flour**, and mix until well blended. Wrap in a plastic bag and chill for three hours.

3. Make filling by snipping **12 ounces of pitted prunes,** combine with 1/2 cup chopped almonds or walnuts, 1/2 cup orange marmalade, 1/2 tsp. cinnamon and 2 Tbsp. fresh lemon juice. Place in a saucepan and cook over low heat a few minutes until thickened.

4. Roll chilled pastry out on a board that has been well sprinkled with **confectioner's sugar.**

5. Cut into 3 inch circles. Place a spoonful of filling in center of each circle and press closed in shape of triangle. Bake on greased cookie sheets 350° until done.

MAPLE HONEY BALLS

1. Drop **2 soft sticks of butter, 4 heaping Tbsp. of honey, 1/2 tsp. maple flavoring** and **1/4 tsp. orange extract** into bowl and mix well.

2. Add **2 cups sifted flour** and a **dash of salt** and mix some more. Mix in **one cup of finely chopped walnuts.**

3. Roll into balls and place on ungreased cooky sheets. Bake about 12 min. in 350° oven until light brown. Remove from pan immediately and drop into a bag filled with **powdered sugar** and shake. Makes 5 dozen cookies.

CHOCOLATE MERINGUE BARS

1. Sift together **2 cups flour, 1/4 tsp. salt, 1/4 tsp. soda,** and **1 tsp. baking powder.**

2. Mix **1 cup soft butter** with **1/2 cup sugar** and **1/2 cup brown sugar** until light and fluffy. Add **2 egg yolks, 3 tsp. water** and **1 tsp. vanilla.** Mix in dry ingredients.

3. Pour in buttered 12" x 8" x 2" pan. Top with **1 six oz. pkg. semisweet chocolate chips.**

4. Beat **2 egg whites** stiff, add **1 cup brown sugar.** Spread over the chocolate.

5. Bake at 350° for 30 minutes. Cut while warm.

TOASTED WALNUT BARS
(Kamish Brodt]

1. Mix together 3/4 cup corn oil, 1 cup sugar, 1 tsp. vanilla and 3 eggs.

2. Add 3 cups flour, 3 tsp. baking powder, 1/2 tsp. salt, and 2 cups chopped walnuts (not too small).

3. Divide dough into balls the size of an orange. Form each ball into a long loaf and roll gently in flour. Place on a cookie sheet or in a shallow pan. Keep adding the balls that have been floured into long and narrow loaves. How many loaves will depend on the length of the pan.

4. Bake at 350° for 45 minutes or until done.

5. When done, cut diagonally while still hot. Then dip each bar into a sugar and cinnamon mixture and place back into the pan. Return pan to turned off oven for 10 minutes.

CHOCOLATE DROP COOKIES

1. Cream 1 1/2 cups brown sugar and 3/4 cup butter. Add 1 egg, 3 tubes (or squares) bittersweet chocolate and beat well.

2. Add 2 1/2 cups sifted flour, 3/4 tsp. soda, 3/4 cup milk, and 1 tsp. vanilla. If desired, add 1 cup crushed nuts.

3. Drop on cookie sheet. Bake at 350° for about 20 to 30 minutes.

4. Frost with fudge frosting.

APRICOT BALLS

1. Mix together 1 large (14 oz.) can sweetened condensed milk, 4 ozs. flaked coconut, and 22 ozs. dried apricots (ground up).

2. Roll into small balls and then roll in powdered sugar. Wet your hands to form into balls. You may freeze until ready to use. Makes about 120 balls.

BROWNIES

1. Melt **1 cup butter** and **3 squares unsweetened chocolate** together in top of double boiler. Cool.

2. Cream **4 eggs, 1 3/4 cups sugar,** and **1 teaspoon vanilla** together. Beat well with chocolate mixture. Add **1 cup sifted flour,** and beat more. Then stir in **1 cup broken walnuts.**

3. Spread in greased 9 × 13 pan and bake about 30 minutes in 350° oven, until surface is firm to touch.

4. Cool and cut in squares. Sprinkle with powdered sugar. Makes 40.

CHOCOLATE PEANUT BARS

1. Mix together **1 cup butter** or **margarine, 1/2 cup white sugar, 1/2 cup brown sugar, 2 egg yolks, 1 tablespoon cold water, 1 teaspoon vanilla, 2 cups flour,** and **1 teaspoon baking soda.**

2. Place in bottom of 10 × 16 greased pan and cover with **1 seven oz. package chocolate chips.**

3. Whip **2 egg whites** until stiff and add **1/2 cup brown sugar.** Spread over top of chips. Spread **1 cup (13 1/2 oz. Planters) whole roasted peanuts** on top.

4. Bake 350° for about 30 minutes. Cut in squares when slightly cool.

CHOCOLATE RUM BALLS

1. **Mix 2 1/2 cups vanilla wafer crumbs, 1 cup confectioners' sugar, 3/4 cup finely chopped pecans** and **2 Tbsp. cocoa** together.

2. Add **1/4 cup rum** and **3 Tbsp. corn syrup** and mix well.

3. With damp hands, roll mixture into 3/4 inch balls. Then roll each ball in **granulated sugar.**

4. Store in tightly closed container. It's better if made ahead a few days before serving. Makes 4 dozen.

INDIVIDUAL JELLY ROLLS

1. Beat **4 egg yolks** until thick and lemon colored.

2. Add **1/4 cup sugar** and **1/2 tsp. vanilla** and beat more.

3. In another bowl beat **4 egg whites** to soft peaks, add **1/2 cup sugar** and beat to stiff peaks.

4. Fold egg yolk mixture into egg whites.

5. To egg mixture add **3/4 cup sifted cake flour, 1 tsp. baking powder** and **1/2 tsp. salt** and fold in gently.

6. Pour into greased and floured jelly roll pan (15 1/2 x 10 1/2 x 1")

7. Bake at 375° for 12 minutes.

8. Loosen sides; turn onto towel sprinkled with sifted confectioners' sugar.

9. Cut cake in half lengthwise. Then cut crosswise in half to make 4 rectangles. Quickly roll up each piece, starting with narrow end; cool.

10. Unroll and spread each with **1/4 cup preserves** of your choice. Reroll; cut each in half to make 2 rolls. Sprinkle with confectioners' sugar. Serves 8.

CHOCOLATE PINWHEEL COOKIES

1. Cream **1/2 cup butter** with **1/2 cup sugar** together until light and fluffy.

2. Add **1 egg yolk** (well beaten) and beat well.

3. Add **1 1/2 cups sifted flour, 1/2 tsp. baking powder, 1/8 tsp. salt** and **3 Tbsp. milk.** Beat until well blended.

4. Divide dough into 2 parts. To one part add **1 square melted bittersweet chocolate** and blend.

5. Chill until firm enough to roll. Roll each half, on wax paper, into a rectangular sheet. On top of chocolate sheet, place plain sheet. Roll as for jelly roll. Chill overnight or until firm enough to slice.

6. Cut in 1/8 inch slices.

7. Bake on an ungreased baking sheet at 400° for five minutes or until done. Makes about 3 dozen cookies.

KIRSBAERKUGLER (DIPPED CHERRY BALLS)

1. Cream 1 stick of soft butter and 1/4 cup powdered sugar. Mix very well. Add 1 and 1/2 cups flour, pinch of salt, and 1 tsp. vanilla.

2. Take a small amount of dough and flatten out in the palm of your hand. Fold dough around a **maraschino cherry**, making a very small ball, or candied cherry.

3. Bake on ungreased cooky sheet 12 to 15 minutes at 350 °.

4. Cool and dip in icing, or **melted sweet chocolate.**

Icing:

1. Mix well together **1 cup sifted powdered sugar, 2 Tbsp. heavy cream,** and **1 tsp. vanilla.**

2. Coat each cherry ball completely in icing. Place on waxed paper to dry.

TOFFEE BARS

1. Beat together **1 stick margarine, 1 stick butter, 1 cup light brown sugar and 1 egg yolk.** Then beat in **2 cups flour.**

2. Pat into a lightly greased cookie pan and bake 20 to 30 minutes at 350°.

3. Melt an **8 oz. milk chocolate candy bar** in double boiler (over water) and spread on baked cooky sheet as soon as pan is removed from oven.

4. Sprinkle with **1 scant cup finely chopped walnuts** and return to turned off oven for 3 minutes.

5. Cut into tiny bars immediately and leave in pan and refrigerate until cold. Makes 7 dozen.

SPRITZ COOKIES

1. Cream 1 cup **soft butter,** 2/3 cup **sugar,** and **3 egg yolks** well.

2. Add 3 cups **cake flour** and 1 tsp. **almond flavoring.** Beat 5 minutes.

3. Fill cookie press and force into desired shape onto ungreased cooky sheet.

4. Bake 8-10 minutes at 400°. Makes 8 dozen cookies.

SOUR CREAM PLUM TORTE

1. In large mixing bowl, place **1 cup sour cream, 1 1/2 cups sugar, 1 stick margarine (or butter), 2 eggs** and beat well.

2. Gently beat in 2 tsp. **baking powder,** 2 heaping cups of **flour** and 1 tsp. **vanilla** and mix well together.

3. Grease loaf pan, 13 x 9, and pour 1/2 of batter in.

4. Spread with **plum preserves.** Pour remaining batter over this and spread on top. Sprinkle lightly with granulated sugar.

5. Bake 350°, 35-45 minutes or until done.

6. Cut diagonally so that pieces of torte will be diamond shaped.

CHOCOLATE TRUFFLES

1. In top of double boiler, over hot water, melt **one 4 ounce package of sweet cooking chocolate,** with **2 Tbsp. milk.** Do not stir. When melted remove from heat and beat in **2 Tbsp. butter.**

2. When cool stir in **1 egg yolk,** and a **few drops of almond flavoring.**

3. Refrigerate until firm. Then shape into small balls, roll **in cocoa or sugar.** Store in refrigerator.

PECAN TASSIES

1. Blend 1 stick (1/2 cup) very soft **butter** and 3 oz. very soft **cream cheese** together.

2. Work in one cup sifted **flour** with a spoon. Chill for an hour.

3. While this is chilling, beat **one egg** with **3/4 cup brown sugar, 1 tablespoon soft butter** and **1 teaspoon orange juice.**

4. Remove cream cheese pastry from refrigerator and shape into 24 one inch balls. Press each ball into a muffin cup, thus forming a pastry cup.

5. Fill each cup with egg mixture by spoonsful. Top with 3/4 cup broken pecans. Bake 325° for 20-25 minutes. Cool, then remove from pan.

CROQUEMBOUCHE

A pyramid of cream puffs decorated to look like a tree with cherries, almonds, and caramel.

1. Place in saucepan, **1 cup water, 1/2 cup peanut oil** (or butter or margarine) and bring it to a fast boil. Remove from heat and stir in **1 cup flour.**

2. Beat **4 eggs** well, add **1/2 tsp. salt** and **1 tablespoon sugar.** Add this to above and stir briskly until smooth.

3. Drop by tablespoon onto greased cooky sheets and bake 425° for 25 minutes. Reduce heat to 300° and bake for 20 to 30 minutes more, or until crisp.

4. When cool, slice partially in half with a sereated knife and fill with **whipped cream that has confectioner's sugar whipped** into it. Makes about 2 1/2 dozen. Make them under 2 inches in size.

5. In another saucepan, place **2 cups granulated sugar,** and add **2 tablespoons water.** Cook over very low heat, stirring constantly, about 10 minutes, until all sugar is melted and light brown colored.

6. Remove pan from stove. Add **1/2 cup very hot water,** very, very slowly. Return pan to stove and cook, stirring constantly, until it turns the color of maple syrup; about 8 minutes.

7. Grease a round serving plate. Make a thin caramelized layer in a circle. Set pan with remaining syrup in a 250° oven to keep soft. Let this circle harden.

8. Remove pan from oven. Dip a portion of each filled cream puff into caramelized sugar, one at a time, and place on the circle of hardened caramel. Keep building up in a decreasing circle to a peak on top. Always be sure the cream puffs are arranged in the outer layers so that their tops form the outside area. Dip **blanched almonds** and drained **maraschino cherries** and fill in occasionally. Reheat the syrup slowly if it should harden too soon.

9. Serve by pulling apart with two forks.

ANISE PUFF COOKIES

1. Beat **3 eggs** until light with 1 cup **sugar**. Add pinch of **salt** and 1/2 tsp. **vanilla** and continue beating.

2. Add 2 cups **pre-sifted flour** to which 1 tsp. **baking powder** has been added. Sprinkle in 1 1/2 Tbsp. of crushed **anise seed**. Beat until well mixed.

3. Line cookie sheets with aluminum foil. Drop by teaspoons a small ammount of dough. About 1/2 teaspoonful. It will flatten to 1 inch in size. Do not place too close together. They should not touch after they have flattened.

4. Place in unheated oven or any place away from a draft, for 10-12 hrs.

5. Bake 325° for about 10-12 minutes until they turn a pale yellow. Do not overbake as they will turn hard. They should be a soft cookie with a puffed glazed top. Makes about 8 dozen. Store in covered tin.

APRICOT CHEESE DELIGHTS

1. Dissolve **one 1 oz. cake yeast** in **1/4 cup scalded milk**, that has been slightly cooled. Add **1 Tbsp. sugar**. Cut **2 sticks butter** into **2 1/2 cups sifted flour**, and **1/2 tsp. salt**. Use a pastry blender as you would for pie.

2. Add **4 egg yolks** to yeast mixture and blend well.

3. Divide dough into two parts. Roll each piece to fit a 13 x 9 pan.

4. Place half in bottom of pan.

5. Beat two **8 oz. cream cheese** with **1 egg yolk, 1 cup sugar**, and **1 tsp. vanilla** until light. Spread over dough in pan. Then spread with **apricot (12 oz. can) cake and pastry filling**.

6. Cut the second piece of dough that has been rolled out into 4 pieces and place on top of apricots. Brush top with sightly beaten **egg white**.

7. Sprinkle **1/3 cup chopped walnuts** over this. Cover and let rise for 2 hours.

8. Bake 350° for 30-35 minutes. When cool, sprinkle with confectioners' sugar. Makes 4 dozen.

OLD FASHIONED HAMENTASHEN

1. In a large bowl place **3/4 cup sugar, 2 cups sifted flour, 2 tsp. baking powder** and **1/4 tsp. salt.**

2. Work **1/2 cup butter** in by hand.

3. Add **1 egg** (beaten) and **2 Tbsp. orange juice.** Mix until dough is formed. Chill overnight if possible, or at least 2 hours.

4. Prepare filling:
   (a) Combine **1 pound pitted and chopped,** unsweetened presoaked prunes with **3 Tbsp. water.** Cook for 10 minutes over low heat.

   (b) Add **1 Tbsp. lemon juice** and **1/2 cup honey.** Cook until thickened, about 5 minutes, stirring frequently.

   (c) Add **2 tsp. lemon rind** and **1/4 cup ground almonds** (or hazelnuts). Mix together.

   (d) Remove from heat and let cool.

5. Roll out dough about 1/8 inch thick on a lightly floured board.

6. Cut into 3 inch circles.

7. Place 1 heaping tsp. of prune mixture on each. Pinch 3 edges of the dough together, but leave a small opening in the center. The resulting pastry will be in the shape of a triangle with a little of the filling showing.

8. Place on a greased cookie sheet. Cover with a cloth and set aside for 1/2 hour.

9. Bake in 400° oven for 20 minutes or until delicately browned on top.

MERINGUE MUSHROOMS

1. Beat **4 egg whites** and **1/4 teaspoon cream of tartar** in large mixing bowl until soft peaks form. Gradually beat in **1 cup sugar** and **1 teaspoon vanilla** until stiff peaks are formed.

2. Spoon onto greased cookie sheet to form mounds about 3 inches in diameter that look like mushroom caps. This should make ten.

3. Spoon the stems on now by making ten 3-inch-long and about 1/4-inch-thick stems. You may use a decorating bag for these.

4. Bake 2 hours and 15 minutes in a 200° oven.

5. When cool, make icing: Mix well **1/4 cup butter, 3 cups powdered sugar,** and **2 tablespoons cream.**

6. Trim with sharp knife so that you may place stems on caps with icing and so that they look like mushrooms.

GRANDMA'S ROLLED COOKIES

1. In large mixing bowl place **¾ cup butter, ½ cup sweet cream (whipping), 1 cup sugar** and **2 eggs.** Beat well.

2. Add **2 teaspoons baking powder** and about **4 cups flour.** Enough flour so that it will roll soft. Mix until smooth.

3. Roll out on a floured board, not too thin, but like a pie shell. Cut with cookie cutters the shapes desired, a little man, rabbit, a chicken, for little children.

4. Place on lightly greased cookie sheets and bake 375° for about 10 minutes.

These are the cookies I watched my Mother make when I was a little girl and loved to eat. Now I am making them for my little granddaughter, Cara Michelle Gordon.

Cakes and Frostings

CAKES AND FROSTINGS

Index

CHOCOLATE BUTTERMILK CAKE

1. Cream 1 1/2 cups sugar and 1 stick butter.

2. Add 2 eggs and 2 pkgs. melted, bittersweet chocolate,(1 oz. squares. Beat well.

3. Dissolve 1 tsp. baking soda in 1 cup buttermilk.

4. Add buttermilk mixture alternately with 1 1/2 cups sifted cake flour. Add 1 tsp. vanilla.

5. Bake in a 9 × 12 loaf cake pan at 350° for 30 to 35 min. Frost when cool. For 3 round 8" pans, bake 325° for 25 to 30 minutes.

PEARL'S CHOCOLATE POUNDCAKE

1. In mixing bowl place 1 3/4 cup sugar, 1/2 pound soft butter and 4 eggs. Beat well.
2. Add 3 tubes or squares melted bittersweet chocolate. Beat well for another minute.
3. Add 3 cups sifted cake flour, 3/4 tsp. cream of tartar, 1/2 tsp. baking soda, 1 tsp. salt, 1 cup milk and 1 tsp. vanilla. Beat slowly until well mixed.

4. Pour into well greased and floured 9" tube pan and bake at 350° for 1 hour or until done. If you use an angel food pan with a removable bottom, do not grease or flour pan.

5. After about 10 minutes, remove from pan.

6. When ready to serve, spoon powdered sugar into ridges on top of cake. Slice thin and serve. If desired, 1/2 cup of very finely chopped nuts may be folded into the batter before baking. Instead of powdered sugar on top, drizzle hot fudge over cake.

SOUR CREAM BUNDT CAKE

1. In a large mixing bowl, cream together 2 1/4 cups sugar, 1 stick of margarine, 1 stick butter, and 6 large eggs.

2. Add 1/2 tsp. salt, 1/4 tsp. baking soda, and 1 cup sour cream and beat more.

3. Add 3 cups sifted regular flour, 2 tablespoons peach brandy, 1 teasp. fresh orange juice and the grated rind of an orange. Beat well.

4. When well blended, pour into a well greased bundt cake pan. Bake in a 350 degree pre-heated oven for 1 1/2 hours or until done.

5. After 10 minutes, go around edge of cake with a knife to loosen. Then let cake cool in pan. Then remove and sift powdered sugar over cake.

PUMPKIN CAKE

1. Cream together **2 cups sugar, 1 cup oil, 3 eggs, 2 cups (16 ozs.) pumpkin, cooked,** and **1 tsp. vanilla.** Beat well.

2. Add **1 tsp. salt, 1 tsp. cinnamon, 1 tsp. cloves, 1 tsp. allspice, 1 tsp. ginger** and **1 tsp. baking soda.** Blend on low speed of your mixer. Gradually add **3 cups sifted flour.**

3. Bake at 350° in a well greased and floured angel food pan for about 1 hour, or until done.

4. Cool well before removing from the pan. **DO NOT INVERT PAN.** Serve with **whipped cream.**

MOTHER'S BIRTHDAY CAKE

1. Cream **3/4 cup butter** and **1 1/2 cups sugar.**

2. Add **3 egg yolks** and beat well.

3. Add **3 cups sifted cake flour, 1 cup milk, 4 tsp. baking powder,** and **1 tsp. vanilla.** Mix well.

4. Fold in **3 stiffly beaten egg whites.**

5. Bake in 3 greased 8" layer cake pans 325° for 30-35 minutes.

6. When cool, frost with the following icing: Mix well **1/4 cup butter, 3 cups powdered sugar, juice of an orange** (or **2 Tbsp. cream**).

SUNDAE BROWNIE CAKE

1. In double boiler melt **1/3 cup butter** and **4 ozs. sweet chocolate.**

2. Cream **4 ozs. cream cheese, 1 cup sugar** and **3 eggs** well.

3. Add melted butter and chocolate, and beat well until smooth.

4. Add a scant **2/3 cup flour, 1 tsp. rum, 1/2 tsp. baking powder, 1/4 tsp. salt** and **1/4 tsp. almond extract.** Mix well until smooth.

5. Add **1/2 cup nuts** if you desire.

6. Pour into greased spring form pan.

7. Bake at 350° for 35-40 minutes.

8. Serve a wedge topped with vanilla ice cream and cover with hot fudge.

ELEGANT BRANDY BUNDT CAKE

1. In large bowl place **1 1/2 cups soft butter, 2 1/4 cups sifted flour, 1/4 tsp. baking soda, 1 1/4 cups sugar** and blend, gently, with **4 Tbsp. peach** (or apricot) **brandy** and **1 1/4 tsp. vanilla.**

2. Add **8 egg yolks** and blend.

3. In another bowl beat **8 egg whites** until frothy; add **1/8 tsp. salt** and **1 cup sugar** and **1 1/2 tsp. cream of tartar.** Beat well until soft peaks form.

4. Gently fold beaten egg whites into cake batter.

5. Pour into a very well greased bundt pan. Gently cut through batter a couple of times.

6. Bake at 300° for 1 hour and 15 minutes.

7. Remove to wire rack and go around pan with knife to loosen. Then hit pan on hard surface. Remove from pan and finish cooling on rack.

8. Before serving, sift powdered sugar over it lightly.

ORANGE CHOCOLATE MARBLE CAKE

1. Preheat oven to 350°

2. Grease pan very well. Do **not** grease if you use an angel food pan with removable bottom.

3. Place **6 oz. semi-sweet chocolate bar** or **semi-sweet chocolate chips** in top of double boiler and melt.

4. In mixing bowl place **3 cups sifted cake flour, 1 tsp. salt, 3 tsp. baking powder, 1 3/4 cups sugar, 1 cup milk, 1/2 lb. butter** (very soft), **1 tsp. vanilla** and **1/2 tsp. orange extract.**

5. Blend these ingredients with mixer at low speed.

6. Add **4 eggs** and beat until smooth. Pour half of batter into another bowl. Add melted chocolate to remaining half and blend well.

7. Spoon the two batters alternately into pan. Cut through batter when pan is filled to marbelize it. Bake 60 minutes. Cool in cake pan 15 minutes, then remove. Sift powdered sugar over cake before serving.

PINEAPPLE UPSIDEDOWN CAKE

1. Melt ¼ cup (½ stick) **butter** in 9×9×1 ¾ inch skillet or pan. Sprinkle ½ **cup brown sugar** over melted butter.

2. Arrange **canned pineapple slices** on top and a **cherry in** in each slice.

3. In large electric mixing bowl place ¾ **cup sugar,** ⅓ **cup butter, 1 egg, 1 teaspoon vanilla** and mix well.

4. Add 1⅓ **cup flour** and ⅔ **cup milk,** and **2 teaspoons baking powder,** and mix until smooth.

5. Pour gently over skillet mixture.

6. Bake at 350° for 40 to 50 minutes. When done invert pan at once, leaving pan over cake for a few minutes. Serve warm.

HONEY CAKE

1. Pour 1 and 3/4 cups **honey** into measuring cup, then into saucepan. Pour 1 cup strong hot **coffee** into same cup and add this to saucepan. Heat to boiling.

2. Remove from heat and add 1 tablespoon of **margarine.** Set aside to cool.

3. When cool add 1 tablespoon **brandy** and 1 tablespoon **peach or apricot brandy.**

4. Meanwhile beat 4 large **eggs** well in a large mixing bowl. Add 1 cup firmly packed **light brown sugar** and beat well.

5. Slowly beat in cooled coffee mixture until well blended.

6. Add **1 1/4 teaspoons cinnamon, 1/4 tsp. nutmeg, 1/4 tsp. ginger, 1/4 tsp. cloves,** and **grated rind of an orange.**

7. Sift **3 1/2 cups all purpose flour,** add **3 tsp. baking powder,** & **1 tsp. baking soda.** Beat in slowly alternately with **1/2 cup white raisins** and **3/4 cup broken walnuts.**

8. Bake in greased 10 inch tube pan at 325 degrees for 1 hour or more until toothpick inserted in cakes comes out clean or when lightly pressed with finger it springs back.

9. Cool in pan. After about 10 minutes go around edge with knife to loosen. Serve glossy side (top) up.

148

ANGEL FOOD CAKE

1. Beat **1 3/4 cups egg whites** (12-14) that have been standing at room temperature. When soft peaks are formed, beat in **1 cup sugar, 1 1/2 tsp. cream of tartar**, and 1/2 tsp. **salt**. Beat until stiff peaks form.

2. Very gently fold in **1 tsp. vanilla extract** and 1/2 tsp. **almond extract** until combined.

3. Add **1 1/2 cups sifted cake flour** and **3/4 cup sifted sugar** and fold in very gently.

4. Spread batter in angel food cake pan and cut through cake.

5. Bake at 375° for 35-40 minutes at lowest rack in oven.

6. When done, invert pan and cool cake at least 2 hours.

NUTMEG CAKE

1. Cream **1 cup butter** and **1 1/2 cups sugar**. Add **4 eggs** and beat well.

2. Add **3 cups sifted all-purpose flour**, 1 1/2 tsp. **baking powder**, 1/8 tsp. **salt**, 1/2 tsp. **mace**, 1/8 tsp. **cloves, 2 tsp. nutmeg**. Pour in 1/2 **cup milk**. Mix gently until well blended.

3. Pour into well greased and floured angel food cake pan.

4. Bake at 350° for one hour. Cool in pan for 15 min. on rack and then remove and finish cooling.

5. When ready to serve, sift confectioners' sugar over cake and fill center with fresh raspberries, fresh strawberries or fresh peaches with confectioners' sugar generously sprinkled over fruit.

CHOCOLATE MOCHA CAKE

1. Cream **1 stick butter** and **1 1/2 cups sugar**. Add **2 eggs** and beat well.

2. Make paste of **4 tsp. cocoa** and **3 Tbsp. hot coffee**.

3. Beat this mixture and add **1 tsp. salt** and **2 cups sifted cake flour**.

4. Dissolve **1 tsp. soda** in **1 cup buttermilk** and mix in. Add **1 tsp vanilla** and mix well.

5. Bake at 350° for 30-40 minutes or until done in a greased loaf pan or in two greased layer pans for 25-30 minutes.

DELICATE ALMOND CAKE

1. Cream **3/4 cup butter** with **1 1/2 cups sugar.**

2. Add **1 1/2 tsp. vanilla, 1/4 tsp. almond extract** and **3 egg yolks** and beat until light.

3. Add**2 1/2 cups sifted cake flour, 3 tsp. baking powder, 1 tsp. salt** and **1 cup milk.** Beat until smooth.

4. Gently fold in **3 egg whites** that have been beaten stiff but not dry.

5. Turn into generously buttered pan (10 inch tube pan) that has **3/4 cup sliced almonds** pressed into butter on bottom and sides of pan, and then sprinkled with **1 Tbsp. sugar.**

6. Bake at 325° for 1 hour or until done. Let cool in pan 15 min., then out of pan on wire rack.

CHOCOLATE ANGEL FOOD CAKE

1. Beat **1 3/4 cups egg whites** (12-14) that have been standing at room temperature. Add **1/2 tsp. salt, 1 1/2 tsp. cream of tartar** and beat until soft peaks form.

2. Beat in **1 cup sugar** and continue beating until stiff peaks form.

3. Gently fold **2 tsp. vanilla** and **1/4 tsp. almond flavoring** into egg whites.

4. Sprinkle **3/4 cup sifted sugar, 1 cup sifted cake flour, 1/4 cup sifted unsweetened cocoa** and fold in very gently.

5. When all ingredients are folded in, gently pour into angel food cake pan and cut through batter.

6. Bake at 375° for 35-40 minutes on the lowest rack in the oven. When done, invert pan and let cool completely—at least 2 hours.

JELLY ROLL

1. Beat **5 egg yolks** and **1 cup sugar** until thick. Add **1 cup flour, 2 teaspoons baking powder, 4 tablespoons cold water, 1 teaspoon vanilla** and beat until blended. Fold in 5 stiffly beaten **egg whites.**

2. Pour batter into a greased 10 × 15 pan that is lined with wax paper. Bake at 375° for 12 to 15 minutes.

3. Sift **confectioners sugar** on a tea towel. When cake is done, tip over onto towel. Peel off paper, trim edges. Whip preserves or **currant jelly** with fork and spread on cake. Roll up and wrap in towel until cool.

BROWN SUGAR ORANGE FROSTING

1. In top of double boiler place **2 egg whites, 1 1/2 cups packed brown sugar** and **1/3 cup water.**

2. Place over gently boiling water and cook for 7 minutes and beat all of the time with an electric mixer.

3. Remove from heat and add **1 tsp. vanilla** and **1/4 tsp. orange extract.** Continue beating untill soft peaks are formed. Spread on cake immediately. Frosts three layer cake.

RUM CAKE

1. Beat **1/2 cup butter, 3/4 cup sugar** and **3 egg yolks** until light and fluffy.

2. Pour in **2 cups sifted cake flour, 2 tsp. baking powder, 1/4 tsp. salt, 1/4 tsp. baking soda, 1/2 cup orange juice, 3 Tbsp. white rum, 1/4 tsp. almond extract** and **1/4 tsp. vanilla extract.** Beat altogether at a low speed.

3. In a separate bowl beat **3 egg whites** until soft peaks form and then add **1/4 cup sugar** and beat until stiff peaks are formed.

4. Fold batter, gently, into egg whites, until well combined.

5. Bake at 350° for 25 minutes in two 9" layer cake pans that have been greased and then lined on the bottom with wax paper.

6. When done, remove from pan and cool on wire rack.

7. Split cooled cake layers crosswise to make 4 layers. Sprinkle each with **2 Tbsps. white rum.**

8. Fill 3 layers with whipped filling.

Whipped Cream Filling

1. Sprinkle **2 tsp. unflavored gelatin** over **2 Tbsps. cold water.** Heat over hot water until gelatin is dissolved, cool slightly.

2. Whip **2 cups cream** with **1/2 cup confectioner's sugar** until fairly stiff. Mix in **1/3 cup white rum.** Add gelatin slowly and beat until it holds shape. Chill in refrigerator immediately and until ready for use.

Chocolate Frosting

1. In mixer place **1 cup confectioner's sugar, 2 tubes** or **squares melted unsweetened chocolate** and **2 Tbsp. hot water.** Beat.

2. Add **2 eggs,** and beat more. Add **5 Tbsp. very soft butter.** Beat until smooth. Frost top and sides of cake.

151

CHOCOLATE SOUR CREAM CAKE

1. In large mixing bowl place **2/3 cup butter, 2/3 cup** (packed) **light brown sugar**, and beat well.

2. Drop in **3 eggs** and beat more.

3. Add **1 cup granulated sugar, 3 tubes** or **squares melted unsweetened chocolate**, and beat until smooth.

4. Add **2 cups sifted cake flour, 1/3 cup Kahlua** (or water), **1 tsp. baking soda, 1 1/2 tsp. baking powder, 1 tsp. salt, 1 cup sour cream** and **2 tsp. vanilla**. Mix until smooth.

5. Pour into two very well greased 9 inch layer pans and bake at 350° for 30 minutes.

6. Cool and frost.

MY DEVIL'S FOOD CAKE

1. In large mixing bowl place **1/2 cup butter, 1 1/4 cups sugar, 2 eggs**

   and **2 tubes** or **squares melted unsweetened chocolate** and beat well.

2. Add **2 cups sifted cake flour, 1 tsp. soda, 1/2 tsp. salt;** pour in **1 cup milk** and **1 tsp. vanilla extract** and mix until smooth.

3. Bake at 350° in greased 9 × 12 loaf pan until cake comes away from the side of the pan, about 30 minutes.

4. Cool in pan on cake rack and frost with Fudge Frosting.

CARROT SPICE CAKE

1. In large mixing bowl place **1 and 1/2 cups granulated sugar** and **1/4 cup light brown sugar, 1 cup oil**, and **4 eggs**. Beat well.

2. Add **2 1/2 cups grated carrots** and beat more.

3. Add **2 tsps. cinnamon, 2 tsp. baking powder, 2 tsps. baking soda, 1/4 tsp. cloves, 1/2 tsp. salt**, and **1/4 tsp. lemon juice**. Beat again.

4. Beat in slowly **2 cups flour** and **1 cup broken walnuts**.

5. Bake in greased angel food pan at 350 ° for 1 hour or until done, when a toothpick in center comes out clean and cake comes away from side of pan. Ice with Lemon Icing when cool.

LEMON ICING

1. Place in mixing bowl **2 Tbsp. very soft butter, 4 ounces very soft cream cheese, juice of half a lemon,** and **2 1/4 cups confectioner's sugar.** Beat until smooth and spread on cake.

HOLIDAY NUT CAKE

1. In large mixing bowl place **3 cups sifted cake flour, 1 3/4 cups sugar, 2 tsp. baking powder, 1 tsp. salt, 1 cup butter** (very soft), **3/4 cup milk,** and **1 tsp. vanilla** and **1 tsp. brandy.**

2. Mix at low speed. Then add **4 eggs** and beat until smooth.

3. Fold in **1 cup** very finely **chopped pecans** or **walnuts.**

4. Grease angel food cake pan unless you have one with removable bottom.

5. Pour in batter and bake at 350° for 1 hour. Cool on rack 30 minutes. Remove from pan.

6. When cool, make a glaze of **2 Tbsp. light corn syrup** and **2 Tbsp. butter.** Boil together for 3 minutes and spoon on top of cake. Place candied cherries on cake before putting on glaze.

WHITE CAKE

1. Cream **1/2 cup margarine** and **1 cup sugar** until smooth.

2. Add **2 cups sifted cake flour, 3 tsps. baking powder, 2/3 cup milk, 1 tsp. vanilla, 1/2 tsp. almond extract** and grated **rind** of a **lemon** and mix well.

3. Beat **3 eggs whites** until stiff but not dry.

4. Fold egg whites into cake batter.

5. Bake at 375° for about 25 to 30 minutes — if you bake in 8 inch layer pans.

6. When cool, remove from pans and frost with White Mountain Creme Frosting (boiled).

7. Add **chopped walnuts** a few cut up **maraschino cherries** and **drained crushed pineapple** mixed with some frosting for the filling.

BURNT SUGAR CHIFFON CAKE

1. In skillet melt **3/4 cup sugar** over low heat, stirring constantly, until brown and smooth. Remove from heat.

2. Slowly stir in **1 cup boiling water;** cook and stir over low heat until lumps dissolve; cool.

3. In a mixing bowl sift **2 1/4 cups cake flour,** add **1 1/4 cups sugar, 3 tsp. baking powder** and **1 tsp. salt.** Make a well in the center. Pour in **1/2 cup cooking oil, 5 egg yolks, 6 Tbsp. water, 1 tsp. vanilla,** and **6 Tbsp.** of the burnt sugar syrup. Beat until very smooth.

4. In large bowl beat **1 cup (about 8) egg whites** and **1/2 tsp. cream of tartar,** until very stiff peaks form.

5. Pour batter in thin stream over entire surface of egg whites. Gently cut and fold just until blended.

6. Bake in ungreased 10″ tube pan 325° for 55 minutes, then at 350° for 10 or 15 minutes. Invert pan and cool cake thoroughly before removing from pan. Frost with the following frosting:

BURNT SUGAR FROSTING

1. In top of double boiler, place **2 egg whites, 1 1/4 cups sugar, remaining burnt sugar syrup, 1/4 cup cold water and a dash of salt.**

2. Beat 1 minute with electric beater. Place over boiling water and cook, beating constantly, until frosting forms stiff peaks, about 7 minutes. Do Not Overcook.

3. Remove from boiling water. Add **1 tsp. vanilla** and beat until of spreading consistency, about 2 minutes. Frost cake!

QUICK APRICOT BRANDY CAKE

1. In large mixing bowl add **1 box yellow cake mix, 1 large pkg. lemon instant pudding mix, 3/4 cup apricot nectar, 2/3 cup salad oil, 4 egg yolks, 1 lemon, juice and rind,** and **1 tsp. apricot brandy.**

2. When all of these ingredients are mixed together, fold in 4 stiffly **beaten egg whites.**

3. Pour into very well greased and floured tube pan (bundt or angel food pan). Grease with Spry or Crisco.

4. Bake at 350° for 1 hour until done.

5. While cake is baking, make the icing: Mix **1 cup confectioners' sugar,** juice of 1 lemon, **1 tsp. apricot brandy.**

6. Spoon this brandy icing over cake while it is still hot — as soon as you remove it from cake pan.

DATE CAKE

1. Cream together **1/2 cup butter** and **1 1/2 cups sugar, 3 eggs less 2 yolks** (these two yolks are reserved for the icing). Beat very well.

2. Add **1 cup sour cream, 1 teaspoon soda, grated rind of half a lemon** and **half of an orange.** Mix well, then add **2 heaping cups of sifted cake flour.**

3. Stir in **1 cup chopped nuts** and **8 oz. fresh dates,** cut up.

4. Pour into greased 9 × 12 loaf pan and bake at 350° until done, probably 30 minutes. It should come away from the side of the pan when it is done.

5. Cool in pan on cake rack. When cool, ice with orange icing.

ORANGE ICING

1. Beat **2 yolks** well, add **rind of 1/2 orange grated** and **2 Tbsp. of orange juice.** Add **confectioners' sugar** to thicken.

2. Beat until smooth and spread on date cake.

DIVINITY FROSTING

1. Combine **1 1/2 cups sugar, 1 Tbsp. light corn syrup,** and **2/3 cup boiling water.**

2. Place over low flame and stir constantly until sugar is dissolved and mixture boils.

3. Continue cooking until a small amount of syrup forms a soft ball in cold water or spins a long thread when dropped from tip of spoon (240°).

4. Pour syrup in fine stream over **2 stiffly beaten egg whites,** beating constantly.

5. Add **1/4 tsp. orange extract** and continue beating until frosting loses its gloss and is stiff enough to spread on cake.

This frosting is tops! It tastes just like divinity!

SNOW PEAK FROSTING

1. Heat **1 1/4 cups white corn syrup** to boiling in small saucepan.

2. With mixer at high speed, beat **2 egg whites** until stiff but not dry: add pinch of **salt.**

3. Slowly pour syrup over beaten whites, continuing to beat until frosting is fluffy and hangs in peaks from beater.

4. Fold in **1 tsp. vanilla.**

This frosting stays soft for at least 2 days.

MARSHMALLOW FROSTING

1. In a saucepan place **1 cup sugar, 1/2 cup boiling water,** and **1/4 tsp. vinegar.** Stir over heat until the sugar is dissolved.

2. Cover for 2 minutes, to prevent crystals from forming and cook without stirring. Remove cover and continue cooking mixture until it forms a softball when a few drops are placed in cold water.

3. Pour in a fine stream over **2 stiffly beaten egg whites.** Beating constantly.

4. Add **10 marshmallows,** quartered, and continue beating.

5. Frost cake. You may sprinkle **coconut** on top if you desire. Use 1 cup moist pack coconut.

FUDGE FROSTING

1. In saucepan place **2 cups sugar, 2/3 cup milk, 2 Tbsp. white corn syrup, 2 tubes melted unsweetened chocolate,** or **squares.**

2. Stir until dissolved. Cook, stirring continuously until it boils.

3. Boil gently, stirring occasionally, until it forms a soft ball when a small amount is dropped in a custard cup of cold water.

4. Remove from heat and add **1 tsp. vanilla** and a large **lump of butter.**

5. Beat with spoon continuously until it gets very thick. Pour over cake.

6. If you desire, sprinkle **walnuts** over frosting.

7. This may be used as regular fudge and poured into a well buttered small pan and when chilled, cut into squares.

BROWN SUGAR BUNDT CAKE

1. Cream together 1 stick soft butter, 2 sticks soft margarine, 2 cups (well packed) light brown sugar, and 6 eggs.

2. Add 3 cups presifted flour, 1 tsp. baking powder and 1/2 tsp. salt. Pour in 1 cup evaporated milk, 2 tsps. maple flavoring and 2 tsp. vanilla. Mix well.

3. Bake 1 1/2 hours, or until done, at 300 °. Frost with Brown Sugar Frosting using evaporated milk.

BROWN SUGAR FROSTING

1. Melt 1 stick butter, stir in 1 cup (packed) brown sugar, and cook for 2 minutes.

2. Let boil, stirring constantly, and add 1/4 cup milk.

3. Bring to a boil, then cool and add 1 3/4 cup powdered sugar and 1 tsp. vanilla.

LEMON ICING

1. Cream 3/4 stick butter, and gradually beat in 1/2 pound powdered sugar.

2. Add 2 1/2 Tbsp. milk and 2 tsp. vanilla and beat until smooth.

3. Add another 1/2 lb. powdered sugar and 2 Tbsp. lemon juice and beat until smooth.

4. Beat in a little yellow food coloring and beat until light and fluffy.

WHIPPED CREAM ICING
(FOR ANGEL FOOD CAKE)

1. Whip 1 pint cream

2. Fold in 1 cup powdered sugar, 1 tsp. vanilla, and 3 Tbsp. cocoa.

3. When smooth and stiff, spread over cake.

Desserts

DESSERTS

Index

DESSERTS

ELEGANT PARTY TORTE

For 2 Layers:
1. Bring **8 egg whites** to room temperature. Add **1 1/2 tsp. vanilla, 1 tsp. cream of tartar, 1 tsp. vinegar** and beat until mixture forms peaks.

2. Gradually add **2 cups sugar.** Beat until mixture is stiff and all of the sugar dissolved.

3. Spread into 2 well greased 9 inch round cake pans. Pans with removable bottoms preferred or line with circle of brown paper and grease sides.

4. Bake at 300° for 1 hour and 15 minutes.

5. Remove from pans immediately and turn onto plates.

6. Whip **1 pint heavy cream** and fold in **#2 can of drained crushed pineapple** and **3/4 cup maraschino cherries,** drained and cut in fourths.

7. Spread between layers and on top and sides just as frosting a cake.

8. Chill overnight in refreigerator.

9. Serves about 8.

For 3 layers:
Use **12 egg whites, 2 tsp. vanilla, 1 1/2 tsp. vinegar, 3 cups sugar** and **1 1/2 tsp. cream of tartar.** (1 1/2 cups egg whites)
Filling for 3 layers:
Use one **#2 can drained crushed pineapple,** and **1 cup cherries** with **1 1/2 pints whipped cream.** #2 can is 2 1/2 cups or 20 ozs.

CHOCOLATE RUM TORTE

Crust:
1. Combine **1 1/2 cups chocolate cookie crumbs, 1/3 cup soft butter** and **1/4 tsp. cinnamon.**

2. Mix well and press with spoon on bottom and sides of 9 inch spring form pan. Bake at 375° for 8 minutes.
Filling:
1. Beat **8 egg yolks** until light. Add **1 cup sugar** and beat some more.

2. Soak **1 Tbsp. gelatin** in **1/2 cup cold water;** place over low flame, bring to a boil, and pour into egg mixture, stirring briskly.

3. Fold in **1 pint cream,** whipped. Then add **1/3 cup dark rum.**

4. Cool until mixture begins to set; pour into chocolate crust. Shave chocolate over top. Refrigerate several hours.

ORANGE SOUFFLÉ

1. Tape a 30" x 6" band of aluminum foil around outside of a 1 1/2 qt. souffle dish. It should stand 4" above rim. Be sure to tape inside and outside seams. Butter inside of foil collar and souffle dish and then sugar, using granulated sugar.

2. Dissolve **2 envelopes unflavored gelatin** in **1/2 cup water.** Stir over hot water until completely dissolved.

3. Place **8 egg yolks** in double boiler top. Add **1/2 cup sugar, 2 Tbsp. lemon rind,** finely grated, **2 Tbsp. orange rind,** finely grated, **1 tsp. salt, 3/4 cup orange juice** and **1/4 cup fresh lemon juice.** Beat until light and fluffy and then cook over water until thick, stirring constantly.

4. Stir in dissolved gelatin. Cool over ice, stir constantly until it begins to mound.

5. Beat **8 egg whites** until frothy. Then beat in **3/4 cup sugar** until soft peaks.

6. Whip **2 cups cream** and pile it on egg whites and fold in custard. Be sure no large areas of white remain.

7. Spoon into souffle dish and refrigerate at least 3 hours or until set.

8. Remove foil when ready to serve. You may garnish with sections of fresh oranges that have been dipped earlier in melted currant jelly or apple jelly. When adding juices, if desired, you may add a few ounces of curacao.

BREAD PUDDING SOUFFLÉ

1. Slice **1 loaf French bread** and place in a large pan. Pour **1 quart (4 cups) milk** over bread and let it soak. Break soaked bread with fork.

2. Beat **5 eggs** with a whisk and add **1 3/4 cups sugar** and beat more. Add **2 tablespoons vanilla** and **1 cup white raisins** and stir into soaked bread.

3. Melt **4 tablespoons (1/2 stick) margarine or butter** in a 350° oven in a 9 × 13 pan. When melted, pour bread mixture into pan. Bake 20 minutes, then turn oven to 400° and bake 40 minutes longer or until firm. Remove from oven.

Brandy Sauce

1. In top of double boiler, place **1 stick butter** and **3/4 cup sugar** and cook until very hot and well mixed.

2. Add **1 beaten egg** and stir in briskly and cook well. Remove from stove and when it cools, add **apricot brandy** or **Cointreau** to taste. Spoon on top of pudding. Place back in oven a few minutes. Serve hot. This is great on a cold snowy night with a fire in the fireplace.

VACHERIN

1. In a large mixing bowl place **8 egg whites** that have been standing at room temperature. Beat until frothy.

2. Add **1 tsp. cream of tartar, 1 tsp. vinegar,** and beat more.

3. Now very slowly pour in **2 cups granulated fine sugar,** beating continuously and very vigorously.

4. Beat in **1 tsp. vanilla** and then continue beating until stiff peaks.

5. Generously grease a spring form pan and the removable bottom only of a round cake pan the same size.

6. Spread 1/4 of the meringue on this separate pan. With a pastry tube, make or spoon kisses on top for decoration. This is the cover.

7. Pour remaining meringue into bottom of spring form pan and, with spoon, spread up the sides to make a shell.

8. Bake at 275° for 1 hour, 15 minutes. Turn off oven and open door and let meringue set in oven for 30 minutes more.

9. Cool thoroughly and then remove to serving plate.

10. Fill any way you desire:
    (a) Strawberry cream made with **2 cups whipped cream, 1 cup sliced fresh strawberries, 1 Tbsp. confectioners' sugar** and **1/4 tsp. almond extract** mixed together.

    (b) **Coffee ice cream** (or any flavor) covered with **whipped cream** with **sliced toasted almonds** and **confectioners' sugar** mixed together.

    (c) **Lemon orange pie** filling topped with **whipped cream.**

    (d) Make a custard: Beat **4 egg yolks** and **1/2 cup sugar** until thick. Beat in **2 Tbsp. water.** Cook in double boiler until custard consistency. Cool and then add **2 tsp. rum.** Pour in Vacherin. Add **1 to 2 cups fresh sliced strawberries** or **peaches.** A little whipped cream should be spread in Vacherin first. Then custard poured in, then fruit, then remainder of whipped cream. Top with **1 cup whipped cream** with **1 Tbsp. Confectioners' sugar** and **1 tsp. of rum** stirred in.

11. Place meringue cover on top of vacherin and serve.

CHOCOLATE MOCHA BAKED ALASKA

Brownie Layer:

1. Melt **1 stick butter** with **2 tubes melted unsweetened chocolate,** stirring constantly over very low heat. Cool.

2. Beat **2 eggs** until light and add **1 cup sugar,** then chocolate butter mixture, **1 tsp. vanilla, 1/2 cup sifted flour** and **1/3 tsp. salt.** If desired, add a **cup of chopped nuts.** Mix well.

3. Bake at 325° for 30 to 35 minutes. When it is done it will be crusty on top. Cool.

4. Place cooled brownie cake on cookie sheet.

5. Line a 1 1/2 quart mold bowl with aluminum foil, leaving an inch extra, or more, to fold back over edge of bowl.

6. Stir **1 quart vanilla ice cream** to soften slightly. Spread a layer an inch thick over bottom and sides of foil lined bowl. Place mold in freezer.

7. Stir **1 quart coffee ice cream** to soften slightly, and pack into center of mold. Cover with foil. Smooth top and freeze.

8. Let ice cream mold stand at room temperature and prepare meringue.

Meringue:

1. Beat **2/3 cup (5 eggs) whites** until soft peaks form. Then gradually add **2/3 cup sugar** and beat until stiff.

2. Remove foil from top of ice cream and invert ice cream mold onto brownie layer. Lift off bowl and peel off foil.

3. Quickly cover ice cream and brownie base with meringue. Swirl into peaks.

4. Bake at once in pre-heated oven. Bake on lowest oven rack in 500° oven and bake 3 minutes or just until meringue is browned.

5. Let stand a few minutes for easier slicing. Cut in wedge shaped slices at table and top with fudge sauce. Serves 12.

165

CHOCOLATE RUM CAKE (ICEBOX]

1. Melt **2 pkgs. sweet chocolate** in top of double boiler, 4 oz. each.
2. Add **3 Tbsp. rum** and blend.
3. Remove from boiling water. Add **2 unbeaten egg yolks,** and beat vigorously until smooth. Add **2 Tbsp. confectioners' sugar** and mix well.
4. Fold in **1 cup heavy cream** that has been whipped, then **2 stiffly beaten egg whites.**
5. Line pan with plastic wrap. I use 1 quart oblong pyrex pan.
6. Separate **ladyfingers** (around 18) and arrange in pan — on bottom and sides. Pour in chocolate mixture. Arrange remaining ladyfingers on top.
7. Chill 12 to 24 hours and then unmold. Makes 8 to 10 servings.

BRANDY SAUCE

1. Combine **1/2 cup sugar, 2 Tbsp. cornstarch,** and **1/4 tsp. salt** in saucepan. Stir in **2 cups boiling water** gradually.
2. Boil for 5 minutes, stirring constantly.
3. Add **1/4 cup butter** and **2 tsp. brandy.**
4. Serve warm on souffle or bread pudding.

CHOCOLATE FONDUE OR HOT FUDGE

1. Melt together **2 giant size milk chocolate candy bars, 1 small jar marshmallow creme,** and **milk** (or cream) in top of double boiler. Stir until smooth. Keep adding more milk until smooth.
2. For fondue, serve hot in fondue dish. Dip: fresh strawberries, ladyfingers or pound cake chunks, banana slices, pineapple chunks.
3. You may drizzle this over chocolate pound cake or orange marble cake or use over ice-cream.

CHOCOLATE ICE CREAM CAKE

1. Combine **4 cups chocolate wafer crumbs** and **1 cup melted butter.**

2. Set 2/3 cup of these crumbs aside.

3. Press remaining crumbs over bottom and up sides of a 9 inch spring form pan. Freeze about 15 minutes or longer.

4. Remove from freezer and spread **1 qt. vanilla ice cream** (softened slightly) over bottom in even layer. Then sprinkle with 1/3 cup of reserved crumbs. Return to freezer until ice cream is firm.

5. Remove from freezer and spread **1 qt. pistachio ice cream,** softened just like in previous step and sprinkle the remaining 1/3 cup of crumbs. Return to freezer.

6. Remove from freezer and spread with **1 qt. of chocolate** (or **strawberry) ice cream.** Cover top of pan with foil and freeze until needed.

7. When ready to serve, first place serving plate in freezer to chill. Make fresh coconut curls with vegetable parer. Refrigerate these.

8. Invert pan onto chilled serving tray. Remove sides and bottom of pan.

9. Garnish cake with coconut curls or flakes. Makes 12 servings.

CHOCOLATE CHEESECAKE

1. Crust: Mix **1 1/2 cups chocolate cookie crumbs, 1/4 cup sugar, 1/4 tsp. nutmeg** and **1/3 cup melted butter.**

2. Press over bottom and up sides (1/2 inch from top) of a 9" spring form pan. Refrigerate.

3. Cake filling: Beat **4 eggs, 1 cup sugar, 3 very soft 8 oz. pkgs. cream cheese.** Add **12 oz. semi-sweet chocolate chips** melted (over hot water). Add **1 tsp. rum** (or vanilla) and **1/2 cup sour cream.** Beat until smooth.

4. Pour into crumb crust. Bake at 350° for 1 hour.

5. Cool in pan on wire rack. Then refrigerate, covered overnight. Remove from pan. Top with whipped cream.

SIMPLY ELEGANT CHEESE CAKE

Crust:

1. In blender finely grind **6 ozs. zwiebach** (1 box).

2. Pour into bowl and add **3/4 cup sugar** and **1 tsp. cinnamon** and mix.

3. Add **1/3 cup melted butter** and mix well together.

4. Press 3/4 of zwiebach mixture into pan. Set 1/4 aside for topping of cheese cake.

Filling:

1. Beat **5 whole eggs** until light.

2. Add **1 1/4 cups sugar, pinch of salt,** and **2 tsp. vanilla,** and beat more.

3. Add **creamed cottage cheese (small curd, 1 large box, 24 ozs.)** and one **8 oz. pkg. cream cheese.**

4. Add **2 1/2 Tbsp. cornstarch.**

5. Add **2 Tbsp. melted butter** and mix well.

6. Put through sieve or food mill.

7. Stir until smooth.

8. Pour into zwiebach shell and sprinkle remaining zwiebach mixture on top.

9. Bake at 350° for 1 1/4 hour or until set.

10. Turn oven off and open door and let remain in oven 1 hour longer or until cooled.

11. When cold, remove from spring form pan and serve.

CHEESECAKE

Crust:

1. Combine **1 1/4 cups crushed graham crackers** or zwiebach, **1/4 cup sugar**, and **1/4 cup melted butter.**

2. Press mixture into spring form pan.

Filling:

1. In mixing bowl place **three 8 oz. pkgs. cream cheese** (very soft), **4 eggs, 1 1/4 cups sugar** and **1 tsp. vanilla.**

2. Cream all ingredients together until very smooth. Pour into graham cracker or zwiebach crust.

3. Bake at 300 ° for one hour.

TOPPINGS:

Cover cheese cake with fresh strawberries. Berries may be cut in half. Melt currant jelly in small saucepan. Spoon melted jelly over each strawberry allowing it to cover cake. Chill and serve.

Blueberry or cherry pie fillings or toppings may be used.

Slice fresh peaches (or use frozen sliced peaches) and arrange on top of cheesecake. Then combine 1/4 cup sugar, 1 Tbsp. cornstarch, 1 Tbsp. lemon juice, and 2/3 cup peach juice in saucepan. Stir and cook over medium heat until thick and clear. Add 1 Tbsp. butter and cook 2 min. Cool, then pour over peaches.

MILK CHOCOLATE SOUFFLÉ

1. Butter a 5-cup soufflé dish and sprinkle with **granulated sugar** on sides and bottom. Fold aluminum foil into thirds to make a 2-inch collar and tape it.

2. In a large skillet, melt **2 tablespoons butter,** stir in **2 tablespoons flour,** and gradually stir in **2 cups milk.** Add **6 oz. milk chocolate candy** or **chips.** Stir constantly until smooth, thick, and comes to a boil.

3. Remove from heat and beat in **4 egg yolks** and **1/4 teaspoon almond extract.**

4. Beat **4 egg whites** until stiff with **1/4 teaspoon cream of tartar** and **1/4 cup sugar.** Fold chocolate mixture into egg whites.

5. Set soufflé dish in large baking pan that has hot water in it.

6. Bake at 350° for 1 hour or until a silver knife inserted in the center comes out clean. Sprinkle lightly with **confectioners sugar.** Serve at once.

INDIVIDUAL MERINGUE SHELLS OR NESTS

1. Beat **3 egg whites**, that are at room temperature, until frothy.

2. Add **1/4 tsp. cream of tartar, dash of salt**, and **1 tsp. vanilla** and beat more.

3. Gradually add **1 cup sugar** and beat until very stiff peaks are formed. Meringue should be glossy, not dry.

4. Draw 8 circles, 3 1/2 inches in diameter on brown paper or foil that is covering baking sheet. Spread each circle with 1/3 cup meringue.

5. Use back of teaspoon and pat center of meringue and mound around edges to make soft peaks.

6. Bake at 275° for 1 hour.

7. Fill meringues with ice cream and sauce or cream filling topped with fresh fruit and whipped cream.

8. To make meringue nests instead of shells, bake meringue in greased individual ramekins or casseroles. Very nice with lemon filling topped with whipped cream and a twist of lemon.

ENGLISH LEMON CHEESE

An English recipe for filling tarts or meringue nests.

1. In double boiler place **3 well beaten eggs, 1/2 cup butter, juice and rind** of **2 lemons**, scant **cup of sugar** and **pinch of salt**. Cook, stirring until thick.

2. Remove from heat and cool. (Keeps well in refrigerator).

3. When ready to fill tarts, beat with a fork and fill.

TAPIOCA PUDDING

1. In saucepan place **6 tablespoons precooked tapioca**, and **6 tablespoons sugar**, **¼ teaspoon salt, 2 egg yolks** and stir.

2. Gradually stir in **4 cups milk**.

3. Cook over medium heat, constantly stirring until it comes to a full boil.

4. While this is cooking beat **2 egg whites**, add **3 tablespoons sugar** and beat until it forms peaks.

5. Slowly pour cooked tapioca into beaten whites beating constantly until fluffy. Beat in **2 teaspoons of vanilla**. Spoon into small dessert dishes. Makes 8 servings. Serve hot or cold.

MERINGUE ROLL

1. Crumble **1 cake yeast**, add **2 Tbsp. sugar** and set aside.

2. Cream **1/2 lb. butter** and **3 egg yolks** well. Add **1/4 cup warm milk, 1 tsp. vanilla** and **2 1/4 cups sifted flour** and mix well. Add yeast mixture and mix. Cover and refrigerate overnight.

3. Beat **3 egg whites stiff** (not dry).

4. Add **3/4 cup sugar** to egg whites and beat.

5. Seperate dough into three parts.

6. Roll out each part of dough (like pie crust) and spread with beaten egg whites. Sprinkle **sugar-cinnamon** mixture over whites (not much sugar). Sprinkle **chopped nuts** over this.

7. Roll up like jelly roll. Sprinkle top with sugar, cinnamon and nuts.

8. Bake at 325° for 40 minutes.

9. Cut into pieces when cool. This may also be made up into individual rolls.

CHOCOLATE ICE CREAM CREPES

1. Beat **2 eggs** untill thick and light. Add **1/4 cup sugar** and beat more. Add **1 tube or square, melted, unsweetened chocolate, 1/4 tsp. cinnamon** and beat more.

2. Pour in **1 1/2 cups milk** and **1/4 tsp. almond extract**.

3. Add **3/4 cup flour** and blend well.

4. Pour **2 Tbsp. batter** into well buttered 7 or 8 inch skillet, tilting pan to coat with batter. Cook, turn once, until browned on both sides.

5. Spoon **1 Tbsp. vanilla ice cream** into center and rool up. Freeze on cookie sheets.

6. Remove from freezer before serving to soften, and top with whipped cream.

CHOCOLATE SOUFFLÉ

1. Generously butter a 2 quart souffle dish. Sprinkle sides and bottom of dish with granulated sugar until coated. Fold a 26 inch piece of aluminum foil or wax paper into thirds to make a 2 inch collar around dish. Tie or tape on.

2. Stir **1/2 cup milk** into **1/2 cup flour, 2/3 cup sugar, 3/4 cup of unsweetened cocoa, 1/4 tsp. salt** and cook, stirring constantly until very thick, gradually adding **1 1/2 cups more milk** and until it comes to a boil.

3. Remove from heat and beat until smooth.

4. Stir in **6 slightly beaten egg yolks** and beat until smooth.

5. Add **2 Tbsp. butter, 1 tsp. vanilla** and beat more.

6. Beat **8 egg whites** until stiff, and beat in **1/4 tsp. cream of tartar,** and **1/3 cup granulated sugar.**

7. Fold in **chocolate mixture** into egg whites, add **1/4 tsp. almond extract.** Pour into soufflé dish. Smooth top of soufflé

8. Set soufflé dish in large baking pan. Pour hot water in pan. Bake in preheated oven 350° for 1 hour, or until done. Test with a silver knife inserted in center comes out clean. You may have to bake 15 minutes longer. Smooth top of soufflé. Sprinkle lightly with **confectioner's sugar.** Serve at once with brandy whipped cream. (**Whipped cream, confectioner's sugar** and **brandy** stirred in.)

FRESH CHERRIES JUBILEE

1. Wash, drain, stem and pit ripe **bing cherries.**

2. Place cherries in kettle. For each cup of cherries use **3/4 cup sugar.** Layer the cherries and sugar, ending up with sugar on top.

3. Let stand 10 to 24 hours in kettle, covered. Then simmer 60 minutes or longer for right consistency. Cook until it thickens.

4. Turn into chafing dish. Slightly warm **cognac** or **brandy** in small pan. Ignite with match; pour over sauce and serve over ice cream.

5. If you wish not to flame or serve in chafing dish, just stir in a little brandy and serve over rich vanilla ice cream.

This is my favorite dessert on a hot summer evening. After step 3, I stir in brandy and pour into sterilized jars and then I have Cherry **Jubilee** to serve over ice cream all year long. This is also excellent served over roast duck.

CHOCOLATE MOUSSE

1. In top of double boiler, beat **4 egg yolks** and **3/4 cup sugar** until thick and lemon colored. Beat in **1/4 cup orange liquor.** Cook over hot, not boiling water, beating constantly until hot and mixture thickens (about 10 minutes).

2. Place top of double boiler in pan of cold water, and beat mixture until very thick (about 5 minutes).

3. Melt **1 six oz. pkg.** of semisweet chocolate chips over hot water. Remove from heat and beat in **1 tsp. instant coffee** that is dissolved in **1/4 cup cold water.** Add **1/2 cup butter,** beat until smooth, then stir in egg yolk mixture.

4. Beat **4 egg whites** with **1/4 tsp. salt** until it forms soft peaks. Add **1 Tbsp. sugar** and beat until stiff.

5. Fold in chocolate mixture. Pour into souffle cups or pots de creme, fill 2/3 full. Cover and chill for 3 hours or more.

6. Serve topped with whipped cream with a little orange liquor and confectioner's sugar in it. Fills 8 cups.

POTS DE CREME

1. In heavy saucepan, combine **1 6oz. pkg. semi-sweet chocolate pieces** and **1 1/4 cups light cream.**

2. Stir over low heat until blended and very smooth. Mixture should be slightly thick—but don't let it boil.

3. Beat **2 egg yolks** with a **dash of salt** until thick. Gradually stir in chocolate mixture.

4. Spoon into 6 or 8 pots de creme cups. Fill 2/3 full.

5. Cover and chill at least 3 hours or until it is thick like pudding.

6. For something different, make lemon-orange filling and pour into Pots de Creme. Top with whipped cream that has confectioners sugar and a taste of rum in it.

LEMON FREEZE

1. Chill 1/2 cup **Pet Evaporated Milk** in ice tray until almost frozen at edges.

2. Mix in 1 quart bowl, 1 egg yolk, 1/3 cup sugar, 1 Tbsp. **lemon juice,** 1/4 tsp. **grated lemon rind** and a few grains of **salt.**

3. Put ice cold milk and 1 **egg white** into cold bowl and mix with cold beaters of electric mixer at high speed until fluffy.

4. Add 2 **Tbsp. lemon juice** and whip until stiff. Beat in sugar mixture gradually at low speed until well mixed. Fills a 1 quart ice tray or 6 small individual dishes.

5. Sprinkle **graham cracker crumbs** on top and freeze until firm — about 3 hours. May garnish with thin slice of lemon cut and twisted.

STUFFED LEMON CREAMS

1. Grate the rind from **2 lemons.**

2. Slice lemons in half and juice.

3. Combine rind, juice and 1 **cup sugar** and stir until sugar dissolves.

4. Pour this mixture into 1 or 2 chilled ice trays and slowly add 1 **pint half and half.** Blend well.

5. Freeze for 2 hours.

6. Cut 4 **lemons** in half lengthwise and remove juice & all pulp.

7. Fill each half with frozen lemon cream, heaping it.

8. Garnish with mint leaf.

CHOCOLATE ROLL

1. In a large mixing bowl beat **4 eggs**, then add **3/4 cup sugar** and beat until very thick and light.

2. Add **2 tubes melted bittersweet chocolate** and beat more.

3. Add **1/2 cup sifted cake flour, 1/2 tsp. baking powder** and **1/4 tsp. salt.**

4. Mix together **2 Tbsp. sugar, 1/4 tsp. baking soda** and **3 Tbsp. milk.** Then add to above mixture and beat at lowest speed on mixer until smooth.

5. Add **1 tsp. vanilla extract** and beat very gently.

6. Bake at 275° for 15 to 20 minutes in a 15" x 10" x 1" jelly roll pan that has been greased and the bottom lined with waxed paper. Cake is done when gently touched with finger and it springs back.

7. When cake is done, loosen edges with knife and turn out on clean towel thickly covered with confectioners' sugar.

8. Peel off paper and trim edges of cake to make rolling easier.

9. Cool cake 5 minutes, then roll up cake with towel in it. Then finish cooling on wire rack.

10. Before serving, beat **1 cup heavy cream** with **1/4 tsp. almond extract.**

11. Unroll cake and spread whipped cream to within 1 inch of each edge. Roll up cake using towel as pusher.

12. Serve and garnish with **maraschino cherries** on the stems which have been dipped first in **hot corn syrup** and then in **chopped nuts.**

BOSTON CREAM PIE

Cake:

1. Sift **2 1/4 cups cake flour** into bowl, add **3 1/2 tsp. baking powder, 1 tsp. salt, 1 1/2 cups sugar.** Drop in **1/2 cup soft butter,** add **2/3 cup milk** and **1 tsp. vanilla.**

2. Beat for 2 minutes.

3. Add **1/3 cup more milk** and drop in **2 eggs.**

4. Beat 2 minutes more.

5. Pour into 2 round paper lined 8 inch layer cake pans.

6. Bake at 350° for 30-35 minutes.

7. When cool, fill with cream filling.

Cream Filling:

1. Mix **5 Tbsp. flour, 1/2 cup sugar,** and **1/2 tsp. salt.**

2. Slowly stir in **2 cups milk,** scalded.

3. Cook in double boiler 15 minutes or until thick.

4. Add a little of hot mixture to **2 slightly beaten eggs.** Stir in remaining hot mixture.

5. Continue cooking 3 minutes. Add **1 tsp. sherry** and **1 tsp. vanilla,** and cool.

6. After filling cake, top with the following chocolate frosting.

Chocolate Frosting:

1. Mix **1/2 cup sugar, 1 1/2 Tbsp. cornstarch, 1 tube** or **square melted, bittersweet chocolate,** and a **dash of salt.**

2. Add **1/2 cup boiling water.**

3. Cook, stirring constantly, until mixture thickens.

4. Remove from heat; add **1 1/2 Tbsp. butter** and **1/2 tsp. vanilla.**

5. Spread on cake immediately.

RUM CHOCOLATE TRIFLE

1. Prepare and bake **1 angel food cake mix** and let cool.

2. Tear cake into pieces and sprinkle cake with **4 Tbsp. rum** and toss lightly.

3. Melt **four 6 oz. pkgs. chocolate chips** over hot water. Turn melted chocolate into mixer bowl and add **6 eggs** (one at a time) and beat.

4. Beat in **2 tsp. vanilla** and a **dash of salt.**

5. Whip **1 pint of cream** until frothy, add **2 Tbsp. sugar** and whip until soft peaks form.

6. Fold cream into chocolate mixture.

7. Layer the cake and chocolate alternately into a 10" tube pan.

8. Refrigerate or freeze until firm.

9. Turn cake out onto serving plate.

10. Whip another **pint of cream** and frost cake.

11. Garnish with **1/4 cup toasted slivered almonds.** Return to freezer. About 30 minutes before serving, remove from freezer to soften slightly. Serves 20.

ENGLISH SHERRY TRIFLE

1. Crumble **sponge cake** or **pound cake** to cover bottom of dish.

2. Soak with equal parts of **sherry** and **pineapple juice,** enough to make fairly moist.

3. Place a layer of drained, cut up **pineapple** (or peaches or pears) over this.

4. Pour **1 pint custard** [not too thick] over fruit.

5. Cover with a thick layer of **whipped fresh cream.**

6. Decorate with **cherries, toasted slivered almonds** or **angelica.**

7. Put in refrigerator for a few hours.

My son Charles Mark brought this recipe from Lancashire, England

RICE PUDDING

1. Mix 1 3/4 cups cooked rice, 1 cup milk, dash of salt, 1/3 cup sugar, 1 tsp. vanilla, 1 well beaten egg, and 1/4 cup raisins.

2. Pour into greased baking dish; dot with butter, and sprinkle sugar and cinnamon on top.

3. Bake at 350° oven 20 minutes or until done.

HAWAIIAN PUDDING

1. In saucepan, combine 2/3 cup precooked rice, 1/2 cup water, 1/4 cup pineapple juice, and 1/2 tsp. salt. Mix until rice is moistened.

2. Bring rice mixture to quick boil, uncovered, fluffing gently with fork. Cover, simmer 3 minutes. Remove from heat and let stand 10 minutes.

3. Add 14 or 16 marshmallows, quartered, (or miniature marshmallow equivalent). Then add 7 or 8 cut up maraschino cherries and an 8 oz. can of crushed, drained pineapple. Cool.

4. Whip 1 cup cream and add 2 Tbsp. powdered sugar.

5. Fold into rice mixture and refrigerate until well chilled. Makes 8 generous servings.

STRAWBERRIES ROMANOFF

1. Lightly sugar 2 quarts hulled strawberries.

2. Whip 1 pint vanilla ice cream slightly.

3. Fold in 1 cup of cream, stiffly beaten.

4. Add 6 full Tbsp. Cointreau Liqueur.

5. Pour mixture over strawberries.

6. Serve either in meringue shells or sherbet glasses.

STRAWBERRY CREAM FLAN

Pastry:

1. Place **2 cups flour, 2 Tbsp. sugar,** and **1/4 tsp. salt** in a bowl.

2. Work in **1 cup soft butter** and **2 egg yolks.** Blend to make smooth dough.

3. Using a double thickness of aluminum foil, make a rectangle 8" x 16" with the two long edges of foil meeting underneath. Roll out pastry on foil until it is identical in shape to the foil. Place on cooky sheet and allow one inch for each side. Stand edges upright to form an oblong pastry case, carefully shaping corners.

4. Chill 1 hour. Prick well with fork.

5. Bake at 425° for 20 minutes or until golden brown.

6. Cool and then remove foil.

Cream Filling:

1. Add **2 Tbsp. confectioner's sugar** to **1 cup whipped cream.**

2. Add **2 Tbsp. light rum** or liqueur.

3. Sprinkle **1/2 cup sugar** and **1/4 cup rum or liqueur** over a **quart of cleaned strawberries.**

1. Spread cream filling in the baked shell and reserve enough to pipe around edge.

2. Arange strawberries in cream close together with points up.

3. Melt **1/2 cup currant jelly** and glaze each berry with it.

4. Pipe remaining cream around edge. Makes **12** generous servings.

BRANDIED CARAMEL FLAN

1. In a large skillet place **3/4 cup sugar**. Cook over medium heat until sugar melts and forms a light brown syrup; stir to blend.

2. Pour syrup immediately into heated 8 inch round shallow baking dish. Tip bowl from side to side to cover bottom and side completely. Set aside.

3. Preheat oven to 325°. Then in saucepan heat **2 cups milk** and **2 cups light cream** until bubbles form around pan's edge.

4. In mixer beat **6 eggs, 1/2 cup sugar, 1/2 tsp. salt**, and **2 tsps. vanilla**.

5. Gradually stir in hot milk and cream and add **1/3 cup peach brandy**.

6. Pour into baking dish that has been prepared. Set dish in a shallow pan and pour boiling water to 1/2 inch level around dish.

7. Bake 40 minutes. Cool, then refrigerate 4 hours or overnight. To serve, run knife around edge. Invert and shake gently to release.

8. Warm **1 Tbsp. brandy** slightly. Ignite and pour over flan. Serves 8.

CANDIED PECANS

1. Combine **1 1/2 cups sugar, 1/4 tsp. salt, 1/4 cup honey** and **1/2 cup water** in saucepan. Cook over medium heat, stirring constantly until sugar is dissolved. Continue cooking, without stirring, to 242° on candy thermometer or until a little in cold water forms a firm ball.

2. Remove from heat and add **1/2 tsp. vanilla** and **3 cups pecan halves**. Stir gently until mixture becomes creamy.

3. Turn onto waxed paper. Separate pecans with fork and let dry.

CANDIED ALMONDS

1. Heat **3 cups dark corn syrup** to 280° (soft crack stage). Do Not Stir syrup while cooking.

2. Remove from heat and quickly stir in **1 cup whole blanched almonds**. Coat each one with candy. Cool until they are just warm.

3. Wet hands and remove coated almonds one at a time. Roll into even shape.

4. Place almonds on waxed paper to harden. Work quickly. This makes 1/2 pound.

FROSTED GRAPES & OTHER FRUITS

Wash and dry fruit. Dip grapes in slightly beaten egg whites. When nearly dry, shake fine granulated sugar over them. For apples, pears, etc. (larger fruits), with your fingers or a brush, coat each fruit with egg white, then roll in sugar and let dry on waxed paper. This makes a beautiful centerpiece in a fruit bowl.

GLAZED MARASCHINO CHERRIES

Dip maraschino cherries on the stem in hot corn syrup. Let dry.

FONDANT FILLED APRICOTS AND PRUNES

1. Combine 1/3 cup butter, 1/3 cup light corn syrup, 1/2 tsp. salt, and 1 tsp. vanilla. Add 1 lb. (one pkg.) confectioner's sugar and mix with spoon until stiff.

2. Turn onto board and knead until well blended and smooth.

3. Fill large pitted prunes and apricot halves. (Use 1 pkg. of apricot halves.) Fill apricot halves with fondant by putting halves together with rounded teaspoon of fondant.

4. Roll prunes and apricots in granulated sugar. Store covered in refrigerator. Makes 4 dozen.

SHERRY ORANGES

1. Cut large oranges in halves and scoop out fruit. Scallop the shells.

2. In a pan add fruit from orange, a large can of crushed pineapple, juice of half a lemon and one heaping Tbsp. of sugar.

3. Cook until it has the consistency of thin marmalade. Add a tsp. of sherry wine.

4. Fill orange shells.

5. Bake at 350° for 20 minutes.

6. Cool and sprinkle top with coconut and serve. Do not place in refrigerator.

WATERMELON ICE

1. Slice **watermelon** in half. Scoop out all melon, just leaving rind.

2. Fill cavity with **raspberry sherbet.**

3. Decorate with chocolate chips so they look like seeds.

4. Refrigerate a short while and serve.

GRAND MARINIER SOUFFLÉ

1. In saucepan melt **4 Tbsp. butter,** and then gradually stir in **3/4 cup flour.** Gradually stir in **3/4 cup milk, 2/3 cup sugar, 1/8 cup fresh orange juice.** Stir and cook until thickened. Cool slightly.

2. With a fork gently beat **5 egg yolks,** then stir into above mixture and beat well. Stir in **1/2 cup Grand Marnier.** Set aside.

3. Beat **8 egg whites** with a pinch of **salt** and **1/8 tsp. cream of tartar,** until stiff but not dry. Gently fold into above mixture with wire whisk.

4. **Butter** and **sugar** a 1 1/2 quart souffle dish. Pour mixture into it. Smooth surface. Bake at 375° for 25 to 30 minutes or until puffed and golden brown. Bake 18 minutes for individual souffles and fill dishes only 3/4 full.

5. Sprinkle with **Confectioner's sugar.** Serve at once.

   Any extra souffle mixture can be warmed in a double boiler over hot water and thinned down with orange juice and a little Grand Marnier and served as a sauce.

PEANUT BRITTLE

1. Place **1 cup brown sugar, 2 cups granulated sugar, 1/2 cup light corn syrup,** and **1/2 cup water** in a 3 quart saucepan. Stir and cook gently.

2. Add **4 tablespoons butter** and stir some more. When it boils, let it cook on medium heat until it reaches 235° on a candy thermometer.

3. Add **2 cups raw Spanish peanuts** (skins and all) and cook until it reaches 290° (hard crack stage).

4. Remove from heat and quickly stir in **1/2 teaspoon soda.**

5. Pour immediately onto two lightly greased cookie sheets. Spread as thin as possible.

6. Loosen edges, pull and stretch thin, then turn when firm. Break when cold.

DIVINITY

1. Place in a 2 quart saucepan, **2 1/2 cups sugar, 1/2 cup white corn syrup,** and **1/2 cup water.** Cook over low heat until sugar dissolves. Cook gently, without stirring to about 265° to 270° on candy thermometer, or until a small amount dropped into a little bowl of cold water forms a firm ball.

2. Beat **2 egg whites** until stiff but not dry. Pour the syrup slowly over egg whites, beating constantly.

3. Add **1/4 teaspoon almond extract** and **a few drops of food coloring** to tint the shade you desire. Add **1/2 cup chopped walnuts** and beat more. When ready, mixture loses its gloss and a small amount holds its shape when dropped from a spoon. Drop by teaspoon onto wax paper. I usually tint my divinity pale pink.

CHOCOLATE DIPPED FRUIT

1. In top of double boiler, over hot water, melt **semi-sweet chocolate chips** or a **bar of sweet chocolate.** Heat to 105° on candy thermometer. Then cool (in a bowl) to 88°.

2. Work on a marble slab and dip in chocolate; **cherries on the stem, pitted prunes, Australian apricots** and **orange peel.**

3. Place directly into paper cups.

ELEGANT CHOCOLATE MOUSSE

1. Dissolve **4 tsp. instant coffee** in **1 pint of whipping cream** that has been chilled. Stir in **4 Tbsp. sugar.**

2. In the top of a double boiler over hot water melt a **4 ounce bar of sweet chocolate.** Remove from heat and water. Cool.

3. Slowly blend in chocolate with coffee and whipping cream. Place in refrigerator and chill mixture before whipping. Whip until stiff. Add **1 tsp. vanilla** and whip in. Spoon into 8 serving dishes and chill until serving.

HOMEMADE ICE CREAM

1. In large mixing bowl beat **8 eggs** until light. Beat in **1 3/4 cups sugar**. Add **1 quart whipping cream, 2 tablespoons vanilla,** and beat until smooth. Gently beat in **3 1/2 cups milk.**

2. Pour into ice cream freezer can that has been chilled. Freeze in your electric or hand freezer until done. Use finely cracked ice. Eight parts ice to one part rock salt.

3. For variations omit vanilla and use fresh lemon juice with a few drops of yellow food coloring. Chocolate that has been grated with almond flavoring. Fresh peaches, fresh strawberries, coffee, or just use your own imagination.

CHOCOLATE CANDY CUPS

1. In the top of a double boiler, over water, melt a **4 ounce bar** of sweet chocolate, add **2 Tbsp. of butter** and stir until smooth. Remove from over water and continue to stir.

2. With a teaspoon, drop chocolate into candy paper cups, then turn around until the entire inside is coated with chocolate. Place candy cups in pan that is a tiny muffin or dessert tin.

3. Chill for 1 hour or until very firm. Fill cups with custard. Peel off paper and garnish with a piece of cherry.

CUSTARD FILLING

1. Melt **2 Tbsp. butter.** Blend **1/4 cup corn starch, 3/4 cup sugar,** and **1/2 tsp. salt.** Add **2 cups milk** gradually. Heat to boiling over direct heat.

2. Stir into **2 slightly beaten egg yolks.**

3. Return to heat and cook 2 minutes. Stirring constantly. Add **1 tsp. vanilla.** When cool fill cups.

BRANDIED BANANAS ZAHAVA

1. Melt **4 tablespoons butter** in chafing dish or skillet. Add **3/4 cup brown sugar, 1/4 cup dark rum, 1/2 cup apricot brandy** and stir and cook until it is blended and thick.

2. Add **2 or 3 bananas** sliced lengthwise and cut 1 1/2 inches long. Sauté in hot brandied mixture. Serve over **French vanilla ice cream** balls at once. (Zahava means gold.)

Beverages and Soups

BEVERAGES AND SOUPS

Index

SUMMER COFFEE PUNCH

1. Make **4 quarts of coffee.** Refrigerate until cold.

2. Whip **1 quart cream,** add 5 Tbsp. sugar and **5 tsp. vanilla.**

3. Place **1/2 gallon of chocolate ice cream** in punch bowl. Pour half of coffee over ice cream; add whipped cream and pour remainder of coffee and mix well. Add cinnamon sticks for flavor.

4. Serves about 50.

FOURTH OF JULY PUNCH

1. Mix **2 cups orange juice, 2 cups lemon juice, 2 cups grenadine syrup.**

2. Pour over ice to chill.

3. When ready to serve, add **2 1/2 quarts chilled ginger ale.** Makes 4 quarts.

DAIQUIRI PUNCH

1. In blender pour **1 bottle daiquiri mix** (16 oz.), **6 Tbsp. superfine sugar, 2 1/2 cups light rum,** 1/2 cup **Curacao** or Cointreau, and **2 dozen ice cubes** (crushed fine) and mix.

2. Pour in **12 oz. Club Soda** and stir.

3. You may use 2 cans of frozen daiquiri mix instead. Serves 20

SUNSHINE PUNCH

1. In large punch bowl combine 1 can [46 oz.] **chilled pineapple juice** and **1 can** [46 oz.] **chilled apricot nectar.**

2. Add **1 quart orange or pineapple sherbet.** Pour **1 quart club soda** over this and serve at once. Makes about 25 to 30 servings.

CHAMPAGNE PUNCH

1. Place ice ring in large punch bowl. Pour **1/4 cup brandy, 1/4 cup Cointreau,** and **1/4 cup light corn syrup** over ice and mix.

2. Add **2 bottles** [fifths] well chilled **champagne, 1 bottle** [fifth] **sauterne,** well chilled, and **1 quart soda water** chilled. (You may leave out sauterne and add 2 bottles soda instead, if desired.) Mix very well.

3. Strawberries and mint leaves frozen in ice ring are the garnish. Makes 4 1/2 quarts or 36 servings.

EGG NOG

1. Beat 1 **dozen egg yolks** until light.

2. Beat **2 cups fine granulated sugar** into eggs.

3. Slowly stir in **1 cup brandy, 1/2 cup peach brandy, 1 cup rum** and **1 quart milk** and pour in punch bowl.

4. Fold in **1 quart whipped cream.**

5. Then fold in **1 dozen stiffly beaten egg whites.**

6. If you desire, you may double the brandy and peach brandy.

7. Top with **nutmeg.** (Freshly grated is the best!)

HOT FRENCH CHOCOLATE

1. Blend **1/2 cup semisweet chocolate chips** with **1/2 cup white corn syrup** and **1/2 cup water** over low heat until chocolate is melted. Pour into small bowl and refrigerate until cool; then add **1 tsp. vanilla.**

2. In large mixer bowl, beat **1 pint heavy cream** and gradually add chocolate mixture. Beat until mixture just mounds. Then spoon into serving bowl and refrigerate.

3. Before serving, scald **2 quarts milk** and pour into heated chocolate or coffee pot and arrange on tray with bowl of chocolate whipped cream.

4. Spoon some chocolate whipped cream into each guest's cup and then fill cup with hot milk. The guest stirs the two together, (with a **cinnamon stick** if desired) before sipping. Serves 16.

WASSAIL BOWL

1. An hour before serving punch, tie in a cheesecloth bag a **1 inch piece stick cinnamon** and **5 whole cloves.**

2. Let this simmer in a large pot in **2 1/2 cups apple cider** with **lemon peel** and **1 tsp. nutmeg** for 15 to 20 minutes.

3. Remove cheesecloth bag, add **3 quarts more cider** and **1 tsp. of vanilla,** and continue to simmer.

4. Serve in punch bowl with **4 small apples** and **1 orange** cut in wedges and not peeled. Add a few whole **cloves** to each orange wedge. The apples and oranges should float on top. Serves about 12.

GAZPACHO

1. Seed **1 green pepper.** Seed and peel **1 large cucumber** and **4 large tomatoes.**

2. Cut up and place in food processor. Add **4 green onions,** (greens and all) sprig of **fresh parsley,** and **2 cloves of garlic,** (put through garlic press), and puree. Do not make too fine.

3. Pour into bowl and add **46 ounces of juice from a can of V8, juice of a fresh lemon, dash of salt, worchestershire sauce** and **white pepper.** Chill and serve cold. Serve with seasoned croutons, if desired.

HOT MULLED CIDER

1. Combine **1/2 cup brown sugar,** and **2 quarts cider.**

2. Tie in small piece of cheesecloth: **1 tsp. whole allspice, 1 tsp. whole cloves, 3 sticks cinnamon,** and **1/4 tsp. nutmeg.** Add this to the cider mixture.

2. Slowly bring to a boil, then cover and simmer 20 minutes.

4. Remove spices. Serve hot with thin slice of unpeeled apple in each glass.

5. Makes 10 servings, so just double for more. Great for "after football party."

JELLIED BEET BORSCHT

1. Dissolve **1 large package lemon jello** in **1 1/2 cups boiling water.** Add **1 1/2 cups beet juice, 1/2 teaspoon sugar,** and **juice of 1 lemon.** Mix well and cool.

2. Beat in **1/2 cup sour cream.** Add **2 cans julienne strips beets** and mix well. Pour into cream soup bowls and chill.

3. Serve with a dab of **sour cream** and with sprig of **watercress.**

JELLIED TOMATO BOUILLON

1. Sprinkle **1 envelope unflavored** gelatin on **1/2 cup of bouillon** to soften.

2. Place over low heat and stir until gelatin is dissolved.

3. Remove from heat and stir in **1/2 cup bouillon** (or consomme) and **1 cup tomato juice, 1/3 cup sherry** and **1 Tblsp. lemon juice.**

4. Pour into soup cups and chill until firm.

5. Break up with fork or cut into cubes before serving.

6. Top jellied bouillon with **sour cream** and **heaping tsp.** of **black caviar,** and serve immediately.

BEET BORSCHT

1. Wash and peel **1 large bunch of fresh beets.**

2. In large kettle place cut up beets and their green tops.

3. Add **one bunch chopped green onions,** including tops.

4. Add **1 thinly sliced carrot** and a **large new potato cut up.**

5. Add water to cover and boil gently until beets, carrot and potato are done.

6. Add a little **sugar** and **lemon juice** to taste.

7. When ready to serve, add a **cup of sweet cream,** or instead of sweet cream, add **sour cream** to each soup cup.

8. Serve hot or cold. Great in hot weather served cold!

CHICKEN SOUP

1. After washing and cleaning **cut up chicken,** place in deep kettle. Fill kettle with **water** covering chicken.

2. Peel and add **one whole onion, two carrots, celery tops, parsnips** (if desired), **salt** and a **little pepper.**

3. Boil gently uncovered for hours until chicken is very tender.

JANET'S FRENCH ONION SOUP

1. Peel and slice **3 large onions.** Sauté gently for 20 minutes in **4 tablespoons butter** and **2 tablespoons of oil** in soup kettle.

2. Meanwhile, brush both sides of **8 French bread slices** with **olive oil** in which **fresh garlic** has been squeezed. Toast in 325° oven, 15 minutes each side, on cookie sheet.

3. In separate pot, heat 2 quarts of well seasoned **beef** and **chicken stock** combined.

4. Stir **3 Tbsp. flour** into onions and add the hot soup stock. Simmer for 30 minutes with kettle cover ajar.

5. Now pour soup into large oven-proof bowl or tureen. Top with toasted French bread slices, and cover completely with large slices of **Swiss cheese.**

6. Place in 375° oven until cheese melts and bubbles.

7. Ladle into bowls at table. Serve with a light salad and ice cold white wine. It's a complete meal! Serves 6.

BEEF SOUP

1. Pour **4 or 5 qts. water** into deep kettle. Add **1 or 2 beef soup bones, 1 whole peeled onion, 2 whole peeled carrots, celery tops** and **salt & pepper.**

2. Rinse **3/4 cup baby lima beans,** add with **1/2 cup or less each of split peas, barley** and **lentils.** Also cut up a **potato** in it.

3. Bring to a boil and simmer for hours uncovered. Serve hot.

VICHYSSOISE

1. Peel **4 large potatoes,** cut in fourths and place in a kettle with **water** to cover. Add **salt,** cover and boil until fork tender.

2. Meanwhile, mince **1 large onion (or 4 or 5 leeks)** and saute' in **6 tablespoons of butter** in a large skillet.

3. Add boiled potatoes and the water they were cooked in. Simmer for about 30 minutes. Add **white pepper** and **salt** to taste.

4. Puree in blender. Gradually stir in **2 cups of milk or cream.** Chill. Serve cold in cream soup cups. Garnish with snipped chives and a sprig of watercress on top.

AFTER DINNER DRINKS

IRISH COFFEE

In an Irish Coffee Cup place 1 cube sugar, 1 jigger Irish Whiskey, pour hot coffee over this to fill cup. Stir, then top with whipped cream.

GRASSHOPPER

In a blender pour equal parts of green Creme de Menthe and white Creme de Cocoa, add ice cream, or ice and whole cream and blend. Serve in champagne glass.

GOLDEN CADILLAC

In a blender place equal parts of Galliano Liqueur, white Creme de Cocoa and whole cream and ice. Blend well and serve in champagne glass.

RUSTY NAIL

Equal parts of Scotch whiskey and Drambuie for the gentlemen.

PINK SQUIRREL

Pour equal parts of white Creme de Cocoa, Creme de Almond, and whole cream into blender. Add ice and blend well. Serve in a champagne glass.

KAHLUA

Pour Kahlua into cordial glass. Pour whole cream onto a teaspoon and "set" cream on Kahlua.

ISRAELI COFFEE

In a tall stemmed cup pour a jigger of Sabra. Fill cup with hot coffee. Top with whipped cream.

AMARETTO di SARONNA

GRAND MARNIER

BRANDY

Passover Cookery

PASSOVER COOKERY

Index

MATZO BALLS #1

1. Beat 4 eggs well. Add 4 Tbsp. water, 4 Tbsp. margarine or chicken fat, 1 tsp. salt and 1/8 tsp. pepper. Add 1 cup Matzo meal. Mix thoroughly.

2. Let stand in refrigerator one hour or more.

3. Wet hands with cold water and form batter into balls. Put in boiling salt water or in chicken soup. Cook 45 minutes to one hour in a covered kettle.

MATZO BALLS #2

1. Beat 3 egg whites until stiff. Set aside.

2. In another bowl, beat 3 egg yolks, 1/2 tsp. salt, and 3/4 cup of matzo meal.

2. Fold in stiffly beaten egg whites. Let stand 5 minutes.

4. Wet hands with cold water and form batter into balls. Put in boiling salt water or in hot chicken soup. Cook 45 minutes in a covered kettle.

FRIED MATZOH

1. Break 2 matzos into pieces about one inch in size. Scald with boiling water and drain immediately.

2. Beat 2 eggs with 1/4 tsp. salt and a dash of pepper. Pour over matzos and toss lightly.

3. Heat butter or margarine in skillet, pour in matzo and egg mixture.

4. Fry until lightly brown on both sides. For fluffly fried matzoh, cover for a few minutes.

5. Serve hot with butter and honey or syrup.

MATZOH PANCAKES

1. Beat **3 egg yolks.** Add **3/4 cup water** and beat in.

2. Add **1/2 cup matzoh meal, 3/4 tsp. salt** and **1 Tbsp. sugar.** Mix well.

3. Let this mixture stand for 30 minutes.

4. Beat **3 egg whites** until stiff. Fold them into the matzo meal mixture.

5. Pour a little **peanut oil** into skillet and heat.

6. Drop batter by tablespoons in skillet and brown on both sides. This recipe makes about a dozen pancakes.

CHAROSIS

1. Pare and core **2 large apples.** Place in blender or food processor with ¾ **cup walnuts.** Chop until fine.

2. Pour into bowl and mix with ½ **teaspoon cinnamon,** ⅛ **teaspoon nutmeg, 1 tablespoon honey** and **1 tablespood red sweet wine.**

MY PASSOVER CAKE

1. Beat **10 egg yolks** until light.

2. Add **1 1/4 cups sugar** and beat well.

3. Add **1/4 tsp. salt, 3/4 cup potato starch, 1/4 cup cake meal,** juice of 1 large **lemon** and **orange juice** to make **1/2 cup of juice** combined.

4. Beat gently until smooth.

5. Fold in **8 egg whites** [stiffly beaten].

6. If desired, fold in **1 cup crushed nuts.**

7. Heat oven to 350°. Bake for 50 to 60 minutes in angel food cake pan.

8. Invert pan until cake is cold.

PASSOVER BANANA CAKE

1. Beat **8 egg yolks**, add **1 cup sugar,** and continue beating until light.

2. Add **1 cup mashed bananas** and beat more.

3. Add 1/4 tsp. salt. 3/4 cup cake meal, 1/4 cup potato starch, and 1 Tbsp. orange juice. Mix well until smooth.

4. Beat **8 egg whites** until stiff. Fold into batter.

5. Gently fold in **3/4 cup crushed walnuts.**

6. Bake at 325° for 45 to 50 minutes in angel food cake pan.

WINE CAKE

1. Beat **12 egg yolks** together with **1 cup sugar** until light.

2. Add **1 cup wine, 1 cup cake meal, 1 tsp. cinnamon** and **1 cup ground walnuts.** Mix well.

3. Fold in **12 stiffly beaten egg whites.**

4. Bake at 325° for 1 hour. Invert pan and cool before removing.

PASSOVER CREAM PUFFS

1. Place in medium size saucepan, **1 cup water** and **1/2 cup peanut oil** and bring to a boil. Remove from heat.

2. Beat **4 eggs** well. Add **1/2 tsp. salt** and **1 cup cake meal** and beat more.

3. Stir this mixture into saucepan of oil and water. Mix until smooth.

4. Drop by tablespoons onto greased cookie sheets and bake at 425° for 25 minutes. Reduce heat to 300° and bake for 30 minutes more, or until crisp.

5. When cool, slice partially in half with a sereated knife, and fill. Makes 20.

ORANGE LEMON FILLING

1. Beat **2 eggs**, then add **3/4 cup sugar** to which **1 Tbsp. potato starch** has been added, and beat more. Pour into a medium size saucepan.

2. Squeeze **1/2 lemon** into measuring cup. Add **orange juice to make 1/3 cup**. Add **2/3 cup water**. Slowly stir this into the egg mixture.

3. Cook over medium heat until it gets very thick, stirring constantly. If desired you may add a teaspoon of **butter**. Remove from heat and cool. Fill cream puffs. You may sprinkle powdered sugar over these before serving.

APPLE ALMOND SOUFFLÉ

1. Crumble **3 matzos** into a large bowl. Pour water over them and let them soak until soft. Drain and squeeze out excess moisture.

2. Beat **6 eggs** until light with **1/2 cup sugar**. Add **1/2 tsp. salt, 1/4 tsp. nutmeg**, and **1/4 tsp. cinnamon** and beat until everything is blended together.

3. Mix in matzos, **1/2 cup ground almonds, 6 apples** that have been peeled and grated, and the **rind of one orange**.

4. Grease and sugar 2 1/2 quart soufflé dish. Pour in ingredients. Sprinkle lightly with a mixture of **cinnamon and sugar**. Then pour **1/4 cup of melted margarine, butter or chicken fat** over this.

5. Bake 350° until brown and firm, about 60 minutes. Serves 8.

PASSOVER POPOVERS

1. Bring **1 1/2 cups water** and **1/2 cup oil** to a boil. Remove pan from stove.

2. Stir in **1/2 tsp. salt, 1 Tbsp. sugar**, and **1 1/2 cups Matzo cake meal**. Stir constantly until it leaves sides of pan clean and forms a ball. Cool.

3. Beat **7 whole eggs** very well. Stir or beat above mixture into beaten eggs.

4. Fill greased muffin tins 3/4 full. Bake 400° for 40 to 50 minutes. Makes 12 large or 18 medium popovers. Serve hot.

CHOCOLATE PASSOVER CAKE

1. Beat **9 large egg yolks** until light. Add **1 1/2 cups sugar** and beat more.

2. Add **1/2 cup orange juice** and **1/2 tsp. almond flavoring**. Add **3/4 cup potato starch, 1/4 cup cake meal** and **4 tablespoons cocoa**. Mix well. Stir in **1/2 cup broken walnuts**.

3. Beat **9 egg whites** well. Fold in mixture to egg whites.

4. Bake 350° for 50 minutes or longer, when cake springs back to your touch. Invert pan until cold.

HORSERADISH

1. Wash and peel **1 horseradish root**. Soak in cold water 1 day.

2. Grate horseradish root (in the fresh air if possible).

3. Add **1/4 tsp. salt**, and **3 Tbsp. of sugar**. Grate a **fresh beet** in and add a little **borsht juice**. Then add **vinegar** (almost a small bottle, the beets and horseradish will absorb the vinegar.

4. Mix several times. Pour into a jar, leaving it uncovered so that it will evaporate and not be too strong. Use with gefilte fish.

GRANDPA'S GESHMIRTE MATZO

1. In large bowl place **16 ozs. large curd cream cottage cheese, 3 heaping Tbsp. sour cream, 3 heaping tsp. sugar, 3 shakes of cinnamon**, and mix well.

2. Beat **one egg** with fork and stir in **1 Tbsp. matzo meal**. Mix until all is smooth.

3. Spread mixture on top of 5 **matzos** that have milk patted on top. Line pan with kitchen parchment.

4. Bake 400° for about 30 to 35 minutes. As soon as removed from oven, sprinkle with **sugar and cinnamon** mixture. Eat warm.

PASSOVER CARROT KUGEL

1. Beat 6 **egg yolks**, add 3/4 cup **sugar** and beat more until thick and light colored.

2. Add 2 cups grated **carrots**, 1/3 cup **matzo meal**, 1/4 cup **potato starch** and 1/2 tsp. **salt**. Mix well

3. Add 1/3 cup **sweet red wine**, 1 Tbsp. fresh **lemon juice** and mix until well belnded.

4. Fold in 6 stiffly beaten **egg whites**.

5. Bake 375° in greased two quart baking dish for 45 minutes. Serve hot.

ALMOND WAFERS

1. Beat 2 **eggs** and l 1/2 cups **sugar** very well.

2. Add 1/2 cup **matzo meal**, 1/2 cup **potato starch**, 1 cup **ground almonds**, and 1/4 cup **peanut oil**. Mix well. Add 1/2 tsp. **almond** flavoring and 1 tsp. **orange peel**.

3. Divide dough in half. Sprinkle potato starch on board and roll each half to 1/8 inch thickness. Cut with two inch cutter and place on lightly greased cooky sheets.

4. Bake at 400° for 10 to 15 minutes or until brown. Makes 4 dozen.

PASSOVER BROWNIES

1. Melt 1 **stick of butter** and mix with 1 **cup sugar**, and 2 **eggs**. Beat well.

2. Add 1/2 cup **cake meal**, 1/4 cup **milk**, pinch of **salt**, 1/3 cup **cocoa**, 1 tsp. **vanilla**, 1/2 cup **chopped walnuts**, and mix well until all is blended together.

3. Bake in greased 8 inch square pan at 350° for 25 to 30 minutes. Cool, then cut into squares.

JELLY ROLL

1. Beat 6 **egg yolks** and 1 cup **sugar** together until light in color. Add grated **rind** and **juice** of half an **orange**. Add 1/2 cup **cake meal** and 1/2 cup **potato starch**, and mix well.

2. Beat 6 **egg whites** until stiff with 1/4 tsp. **salt.** Fold into egg yolk mixture.

3. Line a cookie sheet or an 8" x 12" pan with waxed paper. Spread dough on evenly and bake 325° for 20 to 25 minutes.

4. When done lift out, on the paper and place on a damp cloth. Remove paper. Spread bottom of cake with jelly and roll up. Cut edges off. Leave in damp cloth for 15 minutes so that roll will hold its shape. Dust with powdered sugar. Slice and serve.

INDEX